# THE HOLY LAND
## a personal pilgrimage

by John Weston

# CONTENTS

# CENTRE PLATES

1. The Dome of the Rock and the Golden Gate from the Kidron Valley
2. A Passover in a Rabbi's home in Jerusalem
3. The Mount of Olives
4. The ancient olive trees in the Garden of Gethsemane
5. The rooftops of Bethany
6. The Golden Gate from the Garden of Gethsemane
7. The Church of the Nativity at Bethlehem
8. The road to Emmaus
9. The ruins of Chorazim
10. The Sea of Galilee from the Golan Heights
11. The Negev Desert from Masada
12. The Church of the Annunciation in Nazareth
13. Banyas (Caesarea Philippi) and the source of the River Jordan
14. The statue of Elijah on Mount Carmel
15. The Jezreel Valley from Mount Carmel
16. A boy reading the Old Testament Scrolls

# PERSONAL PROFILE

JOHN ALLEN WESTON , born 1920, son of John and Daisy Weston.

John Weston Senior ministered at Wildfell Hall, Catford, South London for 50 years. The building had been given to him in 1912 by his future father-in-law to serve as a base for his evangelistic ministry.

John Allen lectured in Colleges of Horticulture, and for 15 years was Senior Warden of the Kent Horticultural Institute. It was during this period (1956) that John had a strong desire that Wildfell Hall should become a centre for Bible teaching. It was already an acknowledged centre for evangelistic outreach; it should now feed the Body of Christ in South London. To this end, John coined the title phrase 'The Catford Lectures' and commenced organising monthly Bible addresses. These were initially directed towards local churches who responded in large numbers.

In 1971, he was appointed National Management Training Advisor with the Agricultural Training Board. He was also Senior examiner in Horticultural Management for the City and Guilds of London.

However in 1973, following the tragic death of their son in 1971, John and Margaret moved to Jerusalem to serve with the Churches Ministry to the Jewish People. While in Israel, John was privileged to participate in Agricultural Training programmes organised by the Israeli Ministry of Agriculture.

Later, John joined FEBA Radio, the British missionary radio organisation. He travelled extensively throughout the United Kingdom, Europe, as well as in India, Pakistan and the Seychelles. Apart from various individual broadcasts, including television, John was invited by the BBC to give two series of weekly meditations. He retired from FEBA in 1985 but continued an active Bible teaching ministry, in the United Kingdom, Europe and the U.S.A.

Israel, though, remained his first love. Apart from their 25 years involvement in Holy Land pilgrimages, Margaret and John have led tours in 'The Steps of St Paul' and to 'The Seven Churches' including the Isle of Patmos. This book is based on talks given at the various biblical sites.

# PREFACE

I wish to acknowledge with gratitude, the help and encouragement received from many friends in the compilation of these meditations. In particular is the great spiritual debt I owe to the German Lutheran Evangelical Sisterhood of Mary. This Sisterhood , together with their spiritual Mothers, Mother Basilea (Mb) and Mother Martyria, have been a great source of strength and inspiration. The writings and hymns of Mother Basilea have enriched our lives, as they have done to many thousands across the world.

Shall we ever forget the first two plaques we saw!!? The first stands on Beachy Head, Eastbourne. It reads:

"Mightier than the thunders of many waters, mightier than the waves of the sea, the LORD on high is mighty" (Psalm 93: 4). God is always greater than all of our troubles. Mb

The second is to be seen in the Garden of Gethsemane, and reference is made to it later in this book. We saw both plaques in 1971, but we can still remember the impact they had.

# *INTRODUCTION.*

An Eastern concept, 'Waiting for the Presence', entails waiting in a holy place until the pilgrim hears that 'Still Small Voice' of God speaking. This compilation of gleanings from the Holy Land seeks to share with the reader devotional aspects of some of the holy places. They have been gathered over the past 25 years, covering a period during which we lived in Jerusalem, and then during countless pilgrim journeys. Although it is not a guide book, it comes with a prayer that the reader may be drawn closer in worship, and in service, to the One who made this Land... HOLY.

# 1. JERUSALEM JOURNEY

Onwards and upwards. . . . EL AL. . . . The mighty plane, emblazoned with the Shield of David, ascends higher and higher and then sets its course towards the Holy Land. The Holy Land. . . called thus by the prophet Zechariah - and holy indeed it is. Holy for many reasons. A land set apart for His chosen people. Set apart, too, as the focal point of the universe during the millennial reign of the Messiah. Holy, because it is where the Son of God became incarnate and dwelt amongst us. Especially holy, because it was in this land, that He was crucified, where He shed His precious blood. Oh! holy earth that received that blood as it poured out from His side. Yes, this land is holy.

A grave was opened up to receive His body, but on the third day that grave could no longer keep its prey. Christ had risen and it was from this Holy Land that He ascended into heaven. It will be to this land that He will one day return in majesty. The Holy Land. . . . . a country small in area, but with a significance far exceeding its size. The Holy Land. . . . . . . where, with every footstep, you tread on centuries of history. We recall many happy and joyous occasions: the wedding in Cana, the healing of so many hopeless cases, the glory of the Transfiguration, the celebration of the angels at Bethlehem, and, oh, so many more!

As we walk along its streets, let the stones cry out aloud, telling us of past glories, of past events, reflecting the drama of the Ages. And yet, at the same time, we shall ever be conscious that coming events are casting their shadows before them, and that soon, very soon, in the eternal purposes of God, Israel will take centre stage in world events.

The pilgrim, with Bible in hand, discovers ever new, fresh jewels in this Golden Treasury. . . the Holy Land. After some hours, we cross over the

Israeli coastline. To the right lies Jaffa, the biblical Joppa. It was to here that the prophet Jonah came and took ship in his attempt to get away from obeying the divine commission to go to Nineveh.

Here also lived Tabitha (Dorcas), that woman of good works. It was her death that brought Peter hurrying to Joppa to meet the sorrowing friends. They showed him some of the coats and other clothes that Dorcas had made. Peter puts all the mourners out of the bedroom, kneels down, prays, and calls out, "Tabitha, get up". Dorcas opens her eyes and sits up and Peter then presents her to her friends . . . alive!

It was in the house of Simon the Tanner, at Joppa, that Peter had the vision of 'unclean' creatures and was told by the Lord to kill and eat. "And there came a voice to him, Rise, Peter; kill and eat. But Peter said, Not so, Lord; for I have never eaten any thing that is common or unclean. And the voice spake unto him again the second time, What God hath cleansed that call not thou common" (Acts 11). Three times this vision came and, as Peter pondered over its meaning, a knock was heard. A delegation had arrived from Cornelius, a centurion from Caesarea. This encounter was to lead Peter and the other disciples to realise that the blessing of the Gospel and the gift of the Holy Spirit was to be received by the Gentiles as well as by the Jewish people.

Within minutes of passing Jaffa, the plane lands at Ben Gurion Airport. How can one describe the emotional feeling as we descend from the plane and walk on to the soil of the Holy Land!?! We have arrived in HIS Land. It is an unforgettable experience. The airport is at Lod, the biblical Lydda - important for two main reasons. Firstly, it was here that Peter was visiting when he received the call to Joppa. During his visit, he healed Aeneas, who had been ill for 8 years. Secondly, Lod is the birthplace and burial place of St George, the patron saint of England.

Commencing our journey to Jerusalem, we travel across the southern tip of the Plain of Sharon. Samuel Rutherford, contemplating the heavenly Immanuel's Land, exclaims:-

> There the red rose of Sharon
> Unfolds its heartmost bloom,
> And fills the air of Heaven
> With ravishing perfume.
> Oh! to behold it blossom,

While by its fragrance fanned
Where glory - glory dwelleth
In Immanuel's Land.

Quite near here, we have Modi'n - a new city with an ancient past. Joshua, chasing the Amorites, realised that with the setting of the sun, darkness would quickly fall, thus enabling the enemy to escape.  He calls out to the Lord, and then says in the sight of Israel, "Sun, stand thou still upon Gibeon; and thou, Moon, in the valley of Ajalon. And the sun stood still, and the moon stayed, until the moment of victory" (Joshua 10).

Some scholars believe that Joshua's plea was made from the summit of one of Modi'n's two hills.  A signpost, pointing to Beth Shemesh, indicates that we are close to Samson country, but it was to Beth Shemesh that the Philistines brought the Ark of the Lord.  They had captured the holy Ark and taken it to Ashdod.  They, then, placed it in the temple of their god Dagon, the fish-god.  However, when they discovered, on at least two mornings, their god broken and flat on its face, they were anxious to give the holy Ark back again.  Their desire to do this was increased when the Lord sorely afflicted them. "And the men of Beth-Shemesh said, Who is able to stand before this holy LORD God? and to whom shall he go up from us?  And they sent messengers to the inhabitants of Kirjath-jearim, saying, The Philistines have brought again the ark of the LORD; come ye down, and fetch it up to you" (1 Samuel 6). This they did, and the Ark of the Lord remained at Kirjath-Jearim for 20 years.

As we climb up into the Judean Hills, we see Kirjath-Jearim on our left. We are now coming up to Jerusalem.  The Holy City has been obscured up until now by the topography of the area.  We are unable to catch even a glimpse of it until almost there.

However it will not always be so . . . just listen to the prophecy of Isaiah: "And it shall come to pass in the last days, that the mountain of the LORD's house shall be established in the top of the mountains, and shall be exalted above the hills " (Isaiah 2:2).

A hymn writer in 1764 expressed it so well:

Behold the mountain of the Lord
In latter days shall rise
Above the mountains and the hills
And draw the wondering eyes.

I love verse 3 of this hymn:

The beam that shines on Zion's Hill
Shall lighten every land.
The King who reigns in Zion's tower
Shall all the world command.

Yes, I believe that in that future day, the Holy Hill of Zion will be visible from the coast. How it will cheer and encourage the pilgrims!! For the Christian pilgrim, the journey to Jerusalem is but symbolic of our earthly journey to the Heavenly City:

Come we that love the Lord
And let our joys be known;
Join in a song with sweet accord,
And thus surround the throne.

Then let our songs abound,
And every tear be dry;
We're marching through Immanuel's ground
To fairer worlds on high. (Isaac Watts).

In a sense it could be said that we are living in two time zones. One, the present. The other is a spiritual dimension, described by Paul to the Colossians as having been translated into the kingdom of God's dear Son. In fact, Paul reminds the believers in Ephesus that we have been blessed with all spiritual blessings in the heavenlies.

Jerusalem and the Land of Israel lie before us. We shall discover many pictorial illustrations depicting our heavenly calling. They are there as encouraging milestones on our journey home. Approaching the Holy City, we are filled with a great sense of anticipation. We are entering the only city in the world that has been overshadowed with the divine glory . . . the Shekinah. This glory departed from the city as recorded by the prophet Ezekiel. But this glory will return (Ezekiel 11:23; 43:4).

We instinctively feel that our visit is not only going to be one of truly spiritual significance, but a visit that will also include a spiritual battle. The forces of evil are present here as in no other city. It was in this city that the works of the devil were destroyed. It was in this city that the Lord, having "disarmed the powers and authorities, he made a public spectacle of them, triumphing over them by the cross" (Colossians 2:15, NIV). Satan knows the Bible.   He knows that Jerusalem will be the governmental city of the Messianic reign.   He knows his time is short and so he is doing everything he can to delay the coming of the Messiah.

We bear all this in mind as we come up to Jerusalem.  We always come up to Jerusalem.  When Jewish people immigrate to Israel from the Diaspora, it is described as 'making Alyah'.  This is a Hebrew word meaning 'going up'.

In the Psalms we have the Alyah Psalms - Psalms 120 to 134. 15 Psalms that many believe were sung by the Jewish pilgrims as they travelled up to Jerusalem to celebrate the three great pilgrim Feasts.  At Pesach, Shavuot and Sukkot, the Jewish people were summoned to come before the Lord in Jerusalem. . . and they came with singing.

And so do we!! As we approach the Holy City we break out into song, singing those lovely opening two verses of Psalm 48: "Great is the LORD, and greatly to be praised in the city of our God, in the mountain of his holiness. Beautiful for situation, the joy of the whole earth, is mount Zion, on the sides of the north, the city of the great King."

We have arrived.  The Holy City lies before us.  We recall those Alyah Psalms, and especially Psalm 122: " I was glad when they said unto me, Let us go into the house of the LORD.  Our feet shall stand within thy gates, O Jerusalem...Pray for the peace of Jerusalem".  We bow our heads in silent prayer, and in worship.

Some have suggested that these 15 Alyah Psalms refer to the 15 steps that led from the Court of the Women to the Court of Israel in the holy temple. One step at a time, one psalm at a time.  We too are a kingdom of priests, offering spiritual sacrifices.  Let us take these psalms on our lips as we enter into the Holy City.  A city where our Lord was reviled and rejected, but yet the city where His glory will be made manifest.  The city to which all nations will come to bow down before Him.

Never for one moment think of Jerusalem, of Israel, as museum pieces, where time has stood still.  On the contrary, here is a vibrant city—an exciting land.  Visiting the Holy Land is akin to listening to the music of a glorious symphony.  As you listen, so you interpret the present sound with what has gone before.  This in turn produces the tingle factor; you begin to anticipate the future with pleasurable excitement.  Events from the Old Testament and from the New, all kaleidoscoped together in a most wonderful phantasmagoria of colourful scenes.  Jerusalem awaits us!!! Let us enter the city!!!

# 2. JERUSALEM - THE TEMPLE
# OF THE LORD

Jerusalem...the Old City of Jerusalem, still surrounded by its ancient walls, welcomes us.

In a certain sense we feel as if we have come home. Our base here will be a hotel, aptly named, The Pilgrims Palace. This family hotel is but a stone's throw from the Damascus Gate and is directly opposite the walls of the city.

We leave the hotel and then immediately on our right, facing the walls, we see a hollowed out cave, currently used as a banana warehouse. This in fact is Jeremiah's Grotto. It is traditionally believed that it was here that Jeremiah wrote his Lamentations over the city. The importance of this, from our point of view, is that Jeremiah does not look into heaven and cry to God, "Why does the City sit solitary?" or "Why has she become as a widow?", "Why has she become as a tributary?", "Why has the LORD covered the daughter of Zion in His anger?" (Lamentations 1, 2). No... Jeremiah does not do this, but on the contrary he calls out, "How?", to all these questions.

The Rabbis of old point out that Jeremiah, like Moses in Deuteronomy, never says Why but rather How. Moses says in Deuteronomy 1, "How can I myself alone bear your cumbrance and your burden?" Not "Why should I?"

This is a lesson for us. It so often seems to be our inclination when troubles and tragedies come our way, to cry out "Why, oh why?" to God. Surely the only One who could so address God was our Lord Himself who, in His hour of suffering could cry out, "Lama?", "Why?". For our part, in our moments of crisis, let us call out to the Lord: "How should I respond to this, so as to further your divine will for my life?"

'Thy will be done' blest Lamb divine,
Your prayer in that dark hour,
When facing there the guilt of mine,
God's wrath and Satan's power.

'Thy will be done', redeeming love
Is in these words portrayed,
In perfect trust to God above,
Nor was that trust betrayed.

'Thy will be done', the way seems dark;
Storms sweep across my sky,
I raise my head, your voice to hark
And on your word rely.

'Thy will be done', triumphant Lord!
The grave is empty now,
Vict'ry to me is now assured
If to Your will I bow.

'Thy will be done', O Lord I pray
Teach me that will to know,
That I may follow in the way
That You would have me go.

'Thy will be done', I need the grace
That You alone can give,
By faith I gaze into Your face
Alone for You to live. (J.A.W., 1972).

May we have the strength of purpose to follow the example set by both Moses and Jeremiah.

Walking along a little further, we see a signpost indicating ' Zedekiah's Cave' or 'Solomon's Quarries'. Our gaze is directed to an opening beneath the walls. This is interesting indeed! In the Book of the Kings, we have a graphic account of the building of the first temple. "And the house, when it was in building, was built of stone made ready before it was brought thither:

so that there was neither hammer nor axe nor any tool of iron heard in the house, while it was in building" (1 Kings 6:7).

How this was accomplished was revealed when these underground quarries were found. Heaps of stone chippings were discovered. Here, underground, the stones had been prepared to take their place in the building of the House of the Lord. The work had been done in secret, unseen and unheard by the local population. The first the citizens of Jerusalem knew was when they saw the stones cut and trimmed, ready for their precious task.

What a beautiful picture this is of the work of the Holy Spirit as He prepares the Bride of Christ to meet her heavenly Bridegroom. In Ephesians, we are likened to a building fitly framed together growing into a holy temple in the Lord. Peter declares that we are living stones, built up a spiritual house. How is this being achieved? Surely this is the work of the Holy Spirit in our lives. Secretly done, only the recipients are aware of the chipping and shaping that is being carried out in secret. Painful at times. . . but the result will be glorious!!

We walk on and soon reach the Damascus Gate. This is one of the 8 existing gates in the present city walls. As we pause here, we give a thought to Saul of Tarsus making his way *out* of the city, en route for Damascus. Many believe that it was also *out* of this gate that Stephen was taken for execution. Stephen had that wonderful vision of the Lord in glory as he was about to enter into martyrdom. Saul of Tarsus who had witnessed the martyrdom, was himself to have a vision of the Lord - an encounter on the Damascus road. This was to transform his life and would eventually lead to his martyrdom. The first martyr, the first missionary, both associated here at the Damascus Gate.

We pass through the gate *into* the city , inwardly anticipating that, somewhere on our pilgrim journey, we too may meet the Lord, perhaps not quite so dramatically but it could be equally meaningful. A fairly straight road now takes us directly to the great esplanade that has been opened up before the Western (Wailing) Wall. Here Jewish people come to pray and to lament the destruction of the two temples. Yes, both temples have been destroyed. Although centuries divided both events, they were both destroyed on the *same* calendar date...the 9th of the Jewish month of Av - in Hebrew 'Tisha B'Av', roughly corresponding to August. Nearly all Jewish people believe that this double event was the voice of God speaking to the nation and that it was not just a coincidence of history. On the night of Tisha B'Av, there is much lamenting and the Book of Lamentations is read.

As we stand by the Western Wall, we gaze up to the site of the temple. Here Solomon built his temple, only to be destroyed by Nebuchadnezzar. Then Zerubbabel built a second temple, but it was not to be compared with the magnificence of the former building.    However, the prophet Haggai, acknowledging this fact, proclaims: "I will fill this house with glory, saith the LORD of hosts...the glory of this latter house shall be greater than of the former...in this place will I give peace" (Haggai 2:7,9). How wonderfully and how beautifully this prophecy was to be fulfilled!  Before the second temple was destroyed in AD70, the Prince of Peace, the Creator of the world, our Lord Jesus Himself was to walk within the precincts of this temple.  This indeed was the greater glory - a glory that the first temple never experienced, despite its material splendour.    The glory of the first temple...the greater glory of the second. We now,  with eager anticipation, await the most excellent glory of the Father's House!! (2 Peter 1:17).

Looking up to the Temple Mount, we remind ourselves that this is Mount Moriah, a fact that calls to mind the journey of Abraham and Isaac to this very same mountain top. The question Isaac asks has rung down through the ages: "Where is the lamb for a burnt offering?" and the significant reply of the father: " My son, God will provide himself a lamb for a burnt offering" (Genesis 22).

The centuries pass by, until we hear the call of John the Baptist, as he gazes upon the Lord Jesus, "Behold, the Lamb of God". It was when the Lord as the Lamb of God died on the cross of Calvary, that the great Temple Veil was torn down, from the top to the bottom. The way back to God for sinful man had been opened up.   The writer of the Letter to the Hebrews states: "Having therefore, brethren, boldness to enter into the holiest by the blood of Jesus, by a new and living way which he hath consecrated for us, through the veil, that is to say, his flesh...let us draw near" (Hebrews 10:19,20,22).

Yes, the first two temples have come and gone; we now await the building and completion of the third temple, described for us in the prophecy of Ezekiel. The third temple is inexorably linked with the Messsianic reign and it is for the coming of the Messiah that both Jew and Christian alike await.  A recent headline in the English language daily newspaper, the Jerusalem Post, proclaims, "VERY NEAR THE END" and goes on to say, "There are a growing number of indications that the Messianic Era is about to dawn!" The writer bases his reasoning on a list of signs that were prepared by the Talmudic Sages following their deliberations as to what the world would be like just before the coming of the Messiah.

The Jewish year begins with 7 important months. The first month is a true beginning. It recalls the liberation from Egypt and the fact of Passover. Fifty days later comes the giving of the Law at Sinai - the Feast of Shavuot. As Christians, our beginning is belief in Christ our Passover, and then 50 days later comes our Pentecost and the giving of the Holy Spirit. Just as the Law was given to guide the Israelites through their wilderness journey, so for the believer, the Holy Spirit is given to guide the Church through its journey until the moment of rapture.

The 7th month is the celebration of the in-gathering of the harvest, Sukkot - the Feast of Tabernacles. To the Jew it is no less than entering into the presence of the King of kings - a Palace in Time as it is described by the Sages. In order to prepare for this, the 6th month, 'Elul', is regarded as the month of repentance. It is the vestibule to the Palace, the month of self-preparation. The Hebrew letters for Elul serve as an acronym for the verse in the Song of Solomon: "I am my Beloved's and my Beloved is mine". To the Jew this speaks of the special relationship that exists. How relevant this is to the Christian believer, who awaits with increased expectation the gathering in of the harvest.

The heavenly Feast of Tabernacles, the Marriage Supper of the Lamb, cannot be long delayed. The 7th month begins with the sounding of the ram's horn, the Shofar. The ram's horn is a perpetual reminder to the Jew that on Mount Moriah, but for the ram, the Jewish race would have ceased to be. Our 7th month will also commence with the trumpet sound. Our eternal life is entirely due to the Holy Substitute who took our place, and bore the judgement that was our due. We are surely living in our 6th month, our Elul, the 6th Millennia. This is our time of preparation. Bishop Taylor Smith aptly remarked that "what we weave now, we shall wear then". He was commenting on Revelation 19:7: "Let us be glad and rejoice and give honour to him: for the marriage of the Lamb is come, and his wife has made herself ready".

The Temple Mount, with its third temple, will be the centre of Messianic worship. "And it shall come to pass, that every one that is left of all the nations which came against Jerusalem shall even go up from year to year to worship the King, the LORD of hosts and to keep the feast of tabernacles" (Zechariah 14:16). We recall that the sages of yesterday regarded Jerusalem as the centre of the world, and the temple as the centre of Jerusalem.

We return to our hotel with the distinct feeling that we have been standing on a timebridge, spanning an historic past and an exciting future. We can but echo the closing words of John in the Revelation: "Even so, come, Lord Jesus".

# 3. THE NIGHT OF BETRAYAL

Pilgrims to the Holy Land are often surprised and sometimes confused to find that Calvary is located within the city walls, and the Upper Room is outside. The Church of the Holy Sepulchre, covering both Calvary and the empty tomb, has for a long, long time been engulfed in an expanding city. A further factor has been the re-alignment of the walls. The Upper Room, together with the traditional site of the tomb of King David, were both deliberately kept outside. The builders of the walls, out of spite to both the Jews and the Christians, took this decision. When the Sultan, Suliman the Magnificent, discovered what had been done, in his anger he had the architect executed. In fact, some record that all the builders were similarly dealt with.

Walking through the Old City, we leave by the Zion Gate and make our way to the Upper Room. Here our thoughts turn at once to the Passover meal taken by the Lord Jesus and His disciples. "With desire", He had said, "I desire to eat this Passover with you before I suffer". As we consider the Passover meal, there are three aspects I wish to concentrate upon: the Search - the Seder - and the Psalms.

The Search for leaven prior to the Feast is an essential and very important element. Every house is thoroughly searched to make sure that no trace of leaven has been left undestroyed. Should any be discovered, it is taken outside the house and burnt. Paul, the Jew, recalling this dedicated search, declares that before partaking of the Lord's Supper, a man should examine himself and so let him eat of that Bread and drink of that Cup. To-day, there are many Jewish people who feel that this aspect is taking on a moral dimension as distinct from the practical destruction of the leaven. The importance of this is to allow the eating of the Passover to proceed. It has a positive emphasis, not a negative. This principle must not be overlooked when we meet around the Lord's Table.

The Seder relates to the order that governs the proceedings of the Passover Meal. In this discussion we shall concentrate on the Bread and the Wine. On the Passover Table, there will be three loaves of unleavened bread - the Matzot. Our attention is drawn to the middle Matzah. This is broken in two. Half is eaten and the other half is hidden for the duration of the meal.

If one regards the numeral 3 as symbolic of the Trinity, then the centre loaf corresponds to our Lord Himself. The hidden part represents those hidden years before the commencement of His three years of earthly ministry.

Towards the end of the meal, this hidden part of the Matzah is taken to the Head of the table who then blesses it and all partake of it. It will be the last food to be eaten that night. It was this loaf that the Lord took and said, "This is my body, for you".

In Jewish circles it is explained that as the temple has been destroyed, no lamb can now be sacrificed. Therefore this piece of matzah is eaten as a symbolic reminder of the sacrifice, recalling the lamb that was slain on the night of the institution of the Passover. Hence both Jew and Christian are partaking of exactly the same symbol - the Lamb sacrificed.

During the meal, four ritual cups of wine are drunk and a fifth cup is poured out, but never drunk. The first cup is the cup of Sanctification, drunk at the beginning of the meal. Then part way through the recounting of the deliverance from Egypt, the second cup is taken. This is the cup of Salvation. After the meal has been eaten and the hidden piece of Matzah also eaten, the third cup of wine is drunk. This is the cup of Blessing. It is this cup which our Lord took and declared, "This cup is the new covenant in my blood, which is shed for you". Later the fourth cup, the cup of Thanksgiving, is drunk and the evening draws to a close. The fifth cup, never drunk yet, is Elijah's cup. His presence is eagerly anticipated as his coming is regarded as the harbinger of the Messiah (Malachi 4:5).

These five cups symbolise the expressions of redemption found in Exodus 6:6-8: "I will bring you out...I will rid you out of their bondage...I will redeem you...I will take you to me for a people...I will bring you in unto the land." How precious these promises are to the believer - and in particular the third cup—the cup of Blessing, speaking of redemption.

Just as the Jewish people await the drinking of the fifth cup - so do we await the final aspect of redemption: "I will bring you in".

O what a home! But such His love
That He must bring us there,
To fill that home, to be with Him,
And in His glory share.
The Father's house, the Father's heart,
All that the Son is given,
Made ours, the objects of His love,
And He, our joy in Heaven. (Janetta French)

The late Sir Edward Denny, sums it up in these words:

Oh, if this taste of love
To us is now so sweet,
What will it be, O Lord, above
Thy blessed self to meet?

To see Thee face to face,
Thy perfect likeness wear,
And all Thy ways of wondrous grace
Through endless years declare!

The Psalms are an integral part of the proceedings. During the evening, the six Psalms known as the hallel are sung: Psalms 113-118. They are all so relevant to the Passover. Psalm 118:24 surely finds its true meaning in this night of nights. Night? Yes, but in the divine reckoning, the day of redemption had already begun. The evening and the morning represents the divine order as recorded in Genesis: "And the evening and the morning were the first day" (Genesis 1:5).

We, too, can sing: "This is the day which the LORD hath made; we will rejoice and be glad in it." This the day fore-ordained by God had come. The day the prophets had spoken of, had arrived. The day of man's redemption. A good translation has " Let us rejoice and be glad in Him." How very right this is!!

Having sung these words, and possibly the great Hallel, Psalm 136, the Lord together with His disciples went out into the night and down through the Kidron Valley, making their way to the Garden of Gethsemane. Walking through the valley illumined by the light of a full moon, they pass beneath the shadows of the great temple. Engraved on this temple was a vine. Could it have been this that prompted the discussion outlined in John 15? " I am the true vine". We then have the deeply moving high priestly prayer recorded in John 17.

The drama then moves across the Kidron, and into the Garden of Gethsemane. Here in the very garden where the olives were crushed, the Lord commits Himself to the Father's will. As He contemplates the great work of redemption and all that it entails, He sweats as it were great drops of blood falling down to the ground. In the Garden, a plaque has been placed. We read it in silence:

"O my Father, if it be possible, let this cup pass from me; Nevertheless not my will, but yours be done" (Matthew 26:39). There follows on this plaque the following words:

> You, O Jesus, in Gethsemane
> In deepest night and agony,
> Spoke these words of surrender
> And trust to God the Father.
> In gratitude and love I want to say with You
> In my hour of fear and trouble:
> My Father,
> I do not understand You, but I trust You.   Mb.

As we stand quietly in this most sacred of spots, we recall how an angel came unto Him from heaven, strengthening Him. The sleeping disciples, the motley band, the betrayal by Judas, and then the arrest...all follow. As the officers from the chief priests approach the Lord, He says unto them, "Whom seek ye?" They answered Him, "Jesus of Nazareth". As the Lord utters the words "I AM", I believe all His divine majesty radiated momentarily from His Person. The soldiers, unable to stand before such radiance, went backwards and fell to the ground.

We stand in awe...the Son of man, the Creator of the worlds, He who holds the breath of mankind in His hands, allows Himself to be taken prisoner, and to be led as a Lamb to the slaughter. Taken then to the house of Caiaphas. Here we have a salutary lesson as we observe Peter warming himself by the fire and allowing himself to become involved in a situation that was to lead to his threefold denial of his Master. How we must ever be on guard against the Evil One who constantly seeks to exploit our weaknesses.

What a contrast! Judas, having betrayed the Lord, goes out and hangs himself. Peter, having denied the Lord, repents in tears, receives forgiveness and takes a leading role in the early Church. Little wonder that the emphasis in the Letters to the 7 Churches is on repentance! This call is not to sinners but to Church members who had already repented as sinners.

In the Book of Exodus, we read that the Passover Lamb had to be kept under close surveillance from the 10th day of the first month until the 14th day (Exodus 12:5,6). If, on the 14th day, it was seen to be without blemish, it was then killed. On the first Passover, the blood of the lamb was then placed on the upper doorpost of the house. God declared to the children of Israel: "When I see the blood, I will *pass over* you". Thus those sheltered beneath the blood escaped the judgment of death, that night in Egypt.

Now, here in Jerusalem, we witness the Lamb of God. Christ our Passover, presenting Himself on the 10th day of the first month - a day we call Palm Sunday. Our Saviour was closely watched by the authorities and, on the 14th day, the religious rulers could find no fault and had to resort to hiring false witnesses to uphold their case. Pilate, on that same day, declared, "I find no fault in Him". A statement he made, not once, but three times!

And so it comes to pass, our Passover Lamb is put to death, and His blood is shed. John writes, "The blood of Jesus Christ his Son cleanseth us from all sin".

> Precious, precious blood of Jesus
> Shed on Calvary.
> Shed for rebels, shed for sinners,
> Shed for me.

"When I see the blood" said God, "I will *pass over* you". "This cup", said the Lord Jesus, in the Upper Room, "is the new covenant in my blood, which is shed for you". Anne Steele, the hymnwriter, wrote:

> Blest Lord, what heavenly wonders dwell
> In Thine atoning blood!
> By this are sinners saved from hell,
> And rebels brought to God.

She concludes with words that surely we, too, will want to take on our lips:

What glad returns can I impart,
For favour so divine?
Oh, take me, all, and fill my heart,
And make me wholly Thine.

# 4. THE VIA DOLOROSA

We are now going to retrace the footsteps of Jesus from Pilate's Judgment Hall to the place called Calvary. It will be a journey of poignant memory but a most meaningful one. Let us not get side-tracked by countless speculations that this may not have been the exact route of 2000 years ago. Countless pilgrims have hallowed this Way of the Cross. We are indeed walking along holy ground.

Silently we enter the Old City. The Gate we have chosen to use is known as Herod's Gate, so called because pilgrims in the 16th century believed that a Marmeluke house was in former times a palace of Herod Antipas. Its original name was 'The Flowered Gate.' After a short walk, we reach the beginning of the Via Dolorosa, 'The Way of Sorrows'. This Way has been divided into 14 focal points, known as the Stations of the Cross. Some have a scriptural foundation; others are based on tradition. As we walk, we shall want to pause at each Station and ponder the event represented.

Along the way, there will be much noise and many distractions. However all this will help us to visualise what it must have been like as our Lord passed this way. It was the time of Passover, and Jerusalem was packed with Jewish worshippers from many countries. The noise and bustle must have been just like to-day. The first and second Stations are on the site of the famous Antonia Fortress. Here Pontius Pilate, the Roman Governor, sat in judgment. The first Station is actually in the courtyard of an Arab School; the second, on the road outside the Chapel of Condemnation.

An open gateway attracts our attention, and passing through it we find ourselves in a quiet compound. To the right we see a Chapel; it commemorates the Scourging and the Crowning of Thorns. Over the altar, in the ceiling, there is a beautifully sculptured Crown of Thorns. A Crown of Thorns!!

Was ever a monarch crowned thus? There were no thorns in the Garden of Eden. They were the outcome of man's sin. Jesus, crowned with thorns, was wearing the very symbol of sin. A few yards away is the Chapel of Condemnation. Jesus now receives the cross that He is to carry to the place of execution. We read in Genesis that centuries before, Abraham and his son Isaac were themselves both making their way to this same mountain top. The Bible tells us that the wood was laid upon Isaac as he made his way upwards to the altar of sacrifice.

Before walking down to the third Station, we visit the Convent of the Sisters of Zion. Here we shall see the 2000 year old stones of the original Pavement, the 'Lithostrotos'. Out in the sunshine, we continue our walk down into the Tyropoeon Valley.

We join the road coming from the Damascus Gate. At the junction, we find the third Station, commemorating a tradition that here Jesus stumbled and fell.

The fourth Station, a few yards further on, tenderly suggests that it was here that Mary broke through the crowds and came face to face with her Son. We know that Mary was present at the Crucifixion, but Scripture is silent as to how and where she became aware of the night's events. We take time to think of the sorrow she had anticipated ever since Simeon had so prophesied, 33 years previously, "Sorrow like a sharp sword will break your own heart".

Soon we come to a sharp right turn and the road rises steeply out of the valley, towards the City Gates. Here the Roman soldiers decided that Jesus, weak through loss of blood, had not the strength to carry the cross up the hill on this last part of the journey.

The fifth Station reminds us how Simon of Cyrene was compelled to carry the cross. One wonders if our Lord looked in vain for one or two of those burly fishermen from Galilee to come to His aid.

As we climb this hill we pass the sixth Station. How lovely is the event marked here. How easily it could have happened. I hope it did! A Jewish lady , tradition has it that it was the same lady who had been healed from the issue of blood (Luke 8:43), looking out from her house at the sad procession, saw Jesus in much discomfort. She quickly stepped out and, with a cloth, gently wiped away the sweat and blood from His face. Imagine her surprise, when back indoors, she unfolded the cloth and found an imprint of our Lord's face upon it, so runs the tradition. A true image...Vera Icone...this became her name...and we know her as Veronica.

The seventh Station, in our Lord's day, was at the Gate of the City. It marks the spot where Jesus fell for the second time.

The eighth Station marks the occasion when Jesus turned and spoke to the women of Jerusalem who were watching and crying over His suffering. To reach the ninth Station, we shall have to retrace our footsteps and then continue along the road of the Bazaar until we come to a stone stairway on the right hand side. This will lead us up to the Station that marks the third fall by Jesus.

The remaining Stations of the Cross are all within the confines of the vast Holy Sepulchre Church. This great building spans Calvary as well as the tomb of Joseph of Arimathea. To reach the Church, we have a choice of two routes. We can retrace our footsteps down the stone stairway, making our way around the Russian Hospice , to the door of the Church. The other way, and one that I prefer, is to walk across the roof of the Church, and past the living quarters of the Ethiopian Monks. It is then possible to walk down a very narrow staircase passing their small Chapels, and emerge just by the entrance of the Holy Sepulchre Church.

When Constantine the Emperor adopted Christianity, his mother, Queen Helen, came as a pilgrim to the Holy Land. She had a deep desire to build three great Basilicas: one over the Place of Nativity, one over the Empty Tomb, and one over the Place of Ascension. It was in 335 A.D. that the Church was built over the Tomb of Christ. It was destroyed in 614 A.D. and having been rebuilt, destroyed again in 1009 A.D. The present Church was built by the Crusaders between 1099 and 1149 A.D. The early builders cut away the hillside behind the Tomb, and so left it free standing. It was then adorned with columns, a roof and a porch. Following the destruction in 1009, it was reconstructed, only to be destroyed by fire in 1808. The present Tomb, a replica, was constructed in 1810.

Having entered the Church, we turn to the right and climb up the very steep staircase to the site of the Crucifixion. Here we find Stations 10, 11, 12 and 13. These in turn commemorate the removal of our Lord's garments, the Nailing to the Cross, the Crucifixion, and the taking down of the Body. Confronted by these Stations, we can but kneel down and sing quietly:

> When I survey the wondrous cross,
> On which the young Prince of Glory died,
> My richest gain I count but loss,
> And pour contempt on all my pride.

We sing the whole hymn, for what can we say as we contemplate Calvary. In silence we continue to kneel in worship and thanksgiving. We recall that during the final three hours on the Cross, from midday to three o'clock, there was complete darkness over the land. When Jesus died, an earthquake shook the ground and split the rocks. The seven 'words' from the Cross ring in our ears.

Leaving Calvary, we descend the stairs and make our way to the 14th station, the Tomb of Christ. We have now completed the Stations of the Cross, but here we remind ourselves that with God, for the Christian, suffering is never the end. The grave is empty. Easter Day saw a risen Lord, never to die again. He is alive. He lives to-day as our glorious Lord.

We leave the Church of the Holy Sepulchre, although I prefer to remember it as the Church of the Resurrection. We walk up into Christian Quarter Street, along to David Street. Then turning right we soon reach the Jaffa Gate.

In the distance is the Mount of Olives. One day it is to this mountain that Jesus will return. He will still bear the scars of His passion, but on His head, no crown of thorns, but rather a royal diadem. He will have returned to His City. Peace as never before will spread over the whole earth, and joy to the world!

# 5. BETHANY

Bethany - even to-day, after 2000 years, the very name is evocative. As Mother Basilea says, "the name has a sweet sound to it, conveying love and warmth, speaking of close friends and attentiveness". It proved to be an oasis for our Lord. He found rest there, from the noise and intrigue in the City of Jerusalem. Bethany was the home town of Martha and Mary, and their brother Lazarus.

Christian Churches have existed in Bethany for at least 1600 years. Our first visit is to the Church of St Lazarus surrounded by well kept and beautiful gardens -a modern church built just 30 years ago. Like many of the churches in the Holy Land the accoustics are wonderful for singing and transform a few voices into the sound of a mighty choir!

The Church is beautifully decorated with scenes of the notable events that occurred here. We are reminded of the encounters that Mary, Martha and Lazarus had with the Lord. These special encounters are most significant and speak clearly to us to-day of power, of priorities and of perception.

**Power**

The encounter our Lord had with Lazarus demonstrates the power of the Lord in giving new life. Our Lord's ministry was one of love. The Scripture spells it out so plainly. Before God we are all dead in trespasses and sins. Unable to help ourselves we are faced with a lost eternity. In our helpless situation, our Lord draws near and promises abundant life.

"I am come", He said, "that they might have life, and that they might have it more abundantly" (John 10:10). The Lord brings a message of hope to all mankind.

Many years ago, on holiday on the Isle of Wight, we went out for a walk on to the sands. The tide had just gone out, leaving a glorious stretch of virgin sand. I called a halt, and pointed out to our young children how much our footsteps had spoiled the sand. "Let us smooth them out", I said. They obediently commenced working feverishly until, exhausted and frustrated, they had to admit defeat. In fact the sand surface now looked as if a herd of elephants had trampled over it! Later in the day, the tide came in and went out again. We went to look at the mess we had made...but no sign anywhere. What we had been unable to do, the tide had accomplished perfectly. The sand was as smooth as it was before we had commenced our walk. Our efforts to put our lives aright, only deepen the mess, and leaves us utterly dispirited.

John declares, "The blood of Jesus Christ [God's] Son, cleanseth us from all sin" (1 John 1:7). Toplady in his famous hymn puts it thus:

> Not the labour of my hands
> Can fulfil Thy law's demands;
> Could my zeal no respite know,
> Could my tears for ever flow,
> All for sin could not atone;
> Thou must save, and Thou alone.

The blood of Jesus - this surely is where the power lies. This power is freely available for us to-day.

## Priorities

Martha's encounter with the Lord revealed her need to sort out her life's priorities. We too are so often faced with this urgent task in our own life. The demands of life insist that we have to make decisions for life. Time is a precious commodity . . . a commodity that cannot be saved, cannot be re-lived. It must not be wasted, must not be killed. It is a precious gift that doesn't keep.

The lesson for Martha, and for us, is to strike that right balance. This requires a modicum of discipline. It may mean saying 'No' to some of the requests made of us. It may mean delegating some of our responsibilities. A good idea is sometimes to get out of the woods and look at the trees. All too often we are rushing around and not making effective use of our time.

"Mary", said our Lord, "had chosen the better part". However I do like the little word 'also' to be found in the A.V. (Luke 10:39). It seems to suggest to me that Mary had helped with the chores - but in such a way that she 'also' had time to sit at Jesus' feet. We need that 'also' in our work schedule!!

**Perception**
How beautiful was the perception that Mary had! She had that sixth sense that this would be the last opportunity she would have of expressing her love and devotion to her Lord before His death. Mary drenched the body of our Lord with precious ointment, so much so that the house was filled with the odour of the ointment. Is it not conceivable that, a few days later, our Lord hanging on a cross beneath the burning heat of the sun, might have caught a trace of that perfume? What a beautiful reminder of the worship of one who loved Him and who had expressed it so sacrificially.

One of the most worshipful hymns of Mother Basilea expresses it in such a meaningful manner:

> Balsam I'm bringing
> From deep pain springing,
> Like precious perfume outpouring for You.
> This shall refresh You,
> Comfort, uplift You
> From all the suff'ring sinners inflict.
>
> Love's balsam flowing
> Out of my yearning
> Only to live to bring joy to Your heart.
> Trust when I can't see,
> Trust You entirely,
> This is like costly ointment to You.
>
> I will anoint You,
> Comfort and soothe You,
> With these sweet spices, and love's precious balm.
> Your heart relieving,
> And in its grieving
> Giving refreshment from anguish and pain.

Has this world any
Task that's more worthy,
Task of great glory to serve such a King?
Bring to my Saviour
Comfort and pleasure,
Fall at His feet in homage and love.

Bethany encounters - speaking to us of power, priorities, and perception.

Leaving the Church, we take the ancient road that climbs steeply out of the village, and almost at once come to the entrance to the tomb of Lazarus. Originally the entrance was at ground level, but this is now blocked up, and another one was opened up around 1566. We have to climb down some 24 uneven steps to reach the tomb. Thankfully, electricity was laid on in 1964, enabling us to see clearly both the steps and the tomb itself.

Back in the daylight and the welcoming warmth of the sunshine, we resume our walk towards the summit of the Olivet. After a while we are glad to have a break and, taking advantage of a low wall, we sit down and enjoy the splendid view over the rooftops of Bethany towards the Kidron Valley and beyond. Continuing the journey upwards, we reach the traditional site of the village of Bethphage.

A church commemorates the spot, recalling that this was where our Lord commenced His triumphant entry into Jerusalem on the colt of an ass. If we were here on Palm Sunday, we would witness a great procession of Christians following that same route. The church here in Bethphage is beautiful. The walls and ceiling display a symphony of praise, making a splendid backcloth for the hymns of joyful worship that come spontaneously from our lips.

From Bethphage, it is but a short way, along a good road to the summit of the Mount of Olives. From the summit, a very steep pathway takes us down to the foot, where at the Garden of Gethsemane, we rejoin the main road. Long years ago, the crowds gathered here, with their palm branches, and the singing of their Hosannas, as they witnessed the Lord making His entry into the city. These welcoming cries of 'Hosanna' were soon to change to 'Crucify Him'.

We pause here and look up, over the Kidron, to the Golden Gate, and recall the words of a well known hymn:

And when He comes in bright array,
And leads the conquering line,
It will be glory then to say,
That He's a Friend of mine.


    Yes, Christ is coming again, in Majesty, as the all conquering King, before whom every knee will bow, and every tongue will confess that He is Lord, to the glory of God the Father. Even so, come, Lord Jesus!

# 6. BETHLEHEM

Come, stroll with me along the lanes around Bethlehem. The gentle hills around us are covered with a succession of vine, olive, almond and fig clad terraces. How peaceful they all look. In the winter and spring, the whole countryside is beautifully green. We are some 777 metres above sea level. In the summer, beneath the blazing heat of the Middle Eastern sun, the green disappears and everywhere has a scorched appearance.

As we walk, it is so easy to imagine Ruth and Naomi hurrying along homeward bound, the strong figure of Boaz striding out to the harvest field. The scene changes: it is David leading out a flock of his father's sheep to the rich pasture. He was born here.

As night falls, we can imagine shepherds in these same fields watching their flocks, and being startled beyond measure by heavenly angels celebrating wonderful news. Then in the darkness of earth's long night, they catch a glimpse of the Dawn. The long promised Saviour has come!

As we read the Scripture, it is most interesting to discover the number of events that occur during the night. Abraham went out into the darkness and the Lord told him to look up into the night sky. "Look now toward heaven, and tell the stars, if thou be able to number them: and he said unto him, so shall thy seed be" (Genesis 15:5). Samuel, too, heard the voice of the Lord during the night. Others had dreams and visions.

Perhaps we, too, should be always ready to hear the voice of the Lord during the night-time, particularly on those occasions when, for some seemingly unaccountable reason, sleep deserts us. The shepherds, having heard the message of the angels, hasten into Bethlehem and there they find the Babe. An encounter with Jesus can be a transforming experience, and so it was for the shepherds. They return to their work, praising and glorifying

God and sharing with others the sayings which were told them concerning the Child. Surely they were the first 'broadcasters'!!

The place commemorating the birth of Christ is located beneath the Church of the Nativity. This fortress-like church built on the foundations of Constantine's Church, was constructed by the Emperor Justinian in the 6th century. The essential form of the building has not altered since. It escaped the destruction by the Persians in 614 A.D. It is said that they saw the mosaic representing the wise men, who were depicted wearing Persian clothes, and thought that the church had been dedicated to their gods.

We climb down the short flight of steps to the Grotto. Here we find a shining silver star fitted into the floor of white marble below the altar of the Nativity. Here He was born...we kneel down and lift up our hearts and voices in praise and gratitude before this sublime mystery of love.

> O come, let us adore Him,
> Christ the Lord.

We remind ourselves of the meaning of Bethlehem, 'the house of bread'. Could anywhere else on earth have been the birthplace of the One who is the Bread of Life? He was also that Corn of Wheat, to fall into the ground and die, in order to bring forth much fruit. We further remind ourselves that bread corn must be bruised in order to become flour. Then comes the furnace before bread is produced. "I am the bread of life", said the Lord (John 6:35).

Yes, the shadow of the cross lies heavily over the manger! Some 400 years later, Jerome came to Bethlehem, translated the Old Testament from the original Hebrew, and gave the Vulgate to the world. He is buried below the Church.

Later, we return to the bustling streets above us and recall how, a thousand years before Christ, an embattled David longed for the pure water from the well of Bethlehem. Three of his mighty men fought their way through the Philistine army into the city and brought back the water to their captain.

To-day, Bethlehem is a busy market town, people thronging the streets, dressed in almost every kind of elaborate costume - a town, ancient and modern, side by side. The latest American car alongside a donkey cart! Coffee shops and souvenir shops vie with each other for attention and custom. The main industry is mother of pearl, and lavish supplies of articles are to be found in tempting arrays.   There are also many items in olive wood.

Leaving Manger Square, giving a last lingering glance up to the famous bells, heard throughout the world at Christmas time, we make our way northwards out of the city.   We come to the road fork and join the road coming from Hebron.   Almost at once, our attention is drawn to a white sepulchre beside the main road.   Here is the burial place of Rachel.

Long centuries before Mary and Joseph travelled this road, Jacob and Rachel came this way, hurrying towards Hebron...Rachel expecting her second baby.   It was here, on the outskirts of Bethlehem, that she died in childbirth.   She declared that her baby boy was to be called Ben Oni, 'the son of my sorrow'.   However Jacob decided otherwise and called his name 'Ben Yamin', 'the son of my right hand'.   Benjamin was the only son of Jacob to be born in the Holy Land.   No wonder that the Apostle Paul was proud of his Jewish background - named after the first king of Israel, and born into the tribe of Benjamin!

We hurry on.   Night is falling.   Darkness comes quickly in the Middle East.   As we look back to the city, we see the lights coming on in the houses and shops.   Above, in the clear sky, a solitary star is shining brightly.   It seems to encapsulate all the hopes and fears of not just Bethlehem, but of the whole world.

# 7. EMMAUS

In these gleanings, we are not primarily concerned with the various claims as to the exact location of the original Emmaus. The country hamlet, as portrayed by Mark, has long been lost to posterity.

During the past centuries, four locations have been suggested as being the biblical Emmaus to which the two disciples made their way home on that first Easter Day. These are:

Motza, which is 30 stadia (6km) from Jerusalem, i.e. 60 stadia there and back. Motza was called Emmaus in A.D. 66, but then had a name change to Colonia. Possibly this is why the Byzantines ignored it.

Amwas (Latrun), which is 160 stadia (31km) from Jerusalem. Amwas was recognised by the Byzantines who believed that 100 had been left out of Luke's record. In fact some manuscripts record the distance as being 160 stadia.

El Qubeibeh, which is 60 stadia(11km) from Jerusalem. This site was developed in the 16th century by the Franciscans.

Abu Gosh (Kirjath-Jearim), which is 80 stadia (15km) from Jerusalem. Abu Gosh was favoured by the Crusaders.

It matters not which site has the strongest claim. As far as we are concerned, it is the spiritual aspect and the lessons to be learned which are of greater importance. Having said that, we all have our favourites, mine being El Qubeibeh.

Emmaus…there is not a better example to be found of the ministry of the Good Shepherd than in this event as recorded in Luke 24. It is Resurrection Day…the Lord is risen. The great work of redemption has been completed. The Saviour of the world is alive…to die no more. The disciples are about to be commissioned to take the Good News to the world, but where are they?

The disciples are huddled together in the Upper Room, doors locked for fear of the Jews. They are suffering after all the traumatic events culminating in the trial and crucifixion, convinced that their Divine Master is dead, despite conflicting rumours to the contrary.

The Living Lord knows this, and surely longs to meet with them, to put their troubled minds at rest and to prepare them for the challenge awaiting them. However, this great longing of His heart is overridden by Shepherd love. Two of His disciples have left Jerusalem, in despair, and are on their way home. All during the Shabbat they have been unable to leave. They, too, have heard the rumours. These have only helped to confuse them even more. Finally, rejecting all hope, they leave the rest of the disciples and set off for their village home.

The Lord, the Good Shepherd, assesses the situation. How easy it would have been to have gone straight to the Upper Room and left the other two to their own devices. But no . . . here are two sheep going astray. The Lord leaves Jerusalem, and makes His way along the Emmaus Road. How precious, how gentle is the Shepherd Heart. We hear His questions, as He overtakes them, and their response: "Art Thou only a stranger in Jerusalem?"

How we would have loved to have had a tape recording of the ensuing talk by our Lord Jesus. "Beginning at Moses and all the prophets, he expounded unto them in all the scriptures, the things concerning himself". One can imagine that the conversation made the time and distance just fly by and, before they knew it , there they were at their own garden gate in Emmaus.

How easy it would have been at this stage to have just politely said goodnight to the stranger, and gone indoors and so to bed...and to have missed the blessing. We have here a divine principle. The Lord never imposes Himself on anyone. We see this quite clearly during the storm on the Sea of Galilee, recorded for us in Mark 6:48: "And [Jesus] saw them toiling in rowing; for the wind was contrary unto them: and about the fourth watch of the night he cometh unto them, walking upon the sea, and *would have passed by them*".

Here in Emmaus, how easily this could have happened. But no..."Come in", they said, " Abide with us: for it is toward evening and the day is far spent." And He went in to tarry with them. The Lord never hesitates when a soul invites Him in. Listen to His gracious words: "Behold, I stand at the door, and knock: if any man hear my voice, and open the door, I will come in to him, and will sup with him, and he with me" (Revelation 3:20).

The disciples had left Jerusalem. They had left the Fellowship. How often this finds a reflection in our lives. We make decisions, we go our own way, but our Beloved Lord, the Good Shepherd, ever seeks us, so as to bring us back into the precious communion that we once enjoyed. A meal is prepared - we know the rest. In some special way, the Lord is revealed to them in the breaking of the bread. Was it the manner? Was it a reflection of the Upper Room only three days earlier? Was it the nail prints in His hands? We only have their testimony, "He was known to us in the breaking of bread."

Whatever it was, the effect was electric! At once, all tiredness went, and they rapidly returned to Jerusalem to share the wonderful news with the other disciples. Luke describes the dramatic scene: "They...found the eleven gathered together, and them that were with them, saying, The Lord is risen indeed and hath appeared to Simon. And they told what things were done in the way, and how he was known to them in breaking of bread. And as they thus spake, Jesus himself stood in the midst of them, and saith unto them, Shalom".

Emmaus - the glory of the dawn after the dark night of despair. This cameo speaks to us in so many ways. In our night of sorrow and despondency, when we feel that all hope is lost, Jesus walks with us and brings the radiance of His presence into our gloom.

At El Qubeibeh, there is a plaque for all to read. On it, is printed:

> EMMAUS - The morning dawns.
> EMMAUS - All cares are banished.
> EMMAUS - Our hearts burn within us.
> EMMAUS - Our sorrows have vanished.
> EMMAUS - The Lord has come.
> Jesus, Jesus is here
> To break bread with us. Mb.

In this record of the two disciples on the Emmaus road and that of the parable of the Good Samaritan, we have two precious illustrations of the ministry of the Good Shepherd. In both events, the journey commences in Jerusalem. The one is a picture of lost mankind, made in the image of God but leaving the holy city and going ever further away, down, down on a road that eventually leads to death . . . the Dead Sea.

On this journey there is portrayed the attack of the Evil One, leaving the victim helpless and ready to die. Passing by, come characters representing Religion. One might say, patriarchs, prophets and priests…themselves helpless and unable to relieve the suffering. They simply had not the resources. Then the Stranger appears, the Samaritan, who comes to where the victim is lying. He ministers to him, administers oil and delivers him to the care of the inn, and then promises to return for him. An accurate picture of a world going astray, ever downhill to destruction. A world that has been attacked by Satan, a world that cannot save itself. Wounded and ready to die, a problem to which world religions have no solution.

The Stranger comes, the Lord Himself, bringing with Him all the resources needed to enable Him to save to the uttermost. The wounds are bound up; the oil, symbolic of the Holy Spirit is given, and the rescued victim is left in the care of the Church. A day in the light of heaven is a thousand earth years and the promise is a return in two days. It is now two thousand years since our Lord's return to heaven. Surely His return to earth cannot now be long delayed. This parable is a microcosm of world history and reveals a manifestation of divine grace. It brings a message of hope to mankind.

The Emmaus record shows two disciples and they also are leaving the Holy City. Leaving with a shattered faith. Going not down to the place of death, but rather out into the country, a place of no fellowship and away from the Community in Jerusalem.

"Art thou only a stranger in Jerusalem?" they say to the Lord Jesus as He comes alongside. Here the 'Stranger' has no physical deadly wounds to deal with but rather mental, moral and spiritual wounds resulting from loss of faith. No oil is needed but rather the Word of God and a better understanding of the truth contained in it. The result, the effect, is immediate. "Did not our heart burn within us, while he talked with us by the way, and while he opened to us the scriptures?" they said.

"My sheep know my voice," the Good Shepherd had said. No inn this time, but a home is opened up for closer communion. It is then, in the breaking of bread that their eyes are fully opened, their faith and their joy restored. The outcome of this restoration is the immediate desire to return at once to Jerusalem and to the fellowship of their fellow believers.

In these two vivid pictures - one representing the lost sinner and the other the lost faith - we know only too well that we are so often surrounded by their modern counterparts. The Lord Jesus, the same yesterday, to-day and for ever is always ready to come alongside, to bind up life's wounds and bring complete healing. In the parable, we have one person involved. Thus it must ever be. Each individual is personally responsible and must have a one to one relationship with the Good Shepherd. In Emmaus, we have two, speaking of fellowship and the priority of restoring Christian fellowship where it has broken down. One saved and placed in the care of the Church, awaiting the return of the Saviour. Two, blessed and restored, meeting the Lord as He appears to His own, in their renewed unity . His very first word is "Shalom".

We have considered here the work of the Good Shepherd. We now await the appearing of the Lord as the Chief Shepherd (1 Peter 5:4): "And when the chief Shepherd shall appear, ye shall receive a crown of glory that fadeth not away." Until that day dawns, we are left with a challenge and an exhortation from the Great Shepherd: "Now the God of peace that brought again from the dead our Lord Jesus, that great shepherd of the sheep, through the blood of the everlasting covenant, make you perfect in every good work to do his will, working in you that which is pleasing in his sight through Jesus Christ; to whom be glory for ever and ever. Amen" (Hebrews 13:20,21).

# 8. THE SEA OF GALILEE.

Many seas have been created - but of all those seas, the one so beloved by the Creator and by countless generations, is surely the Sea of Galilee. Known in Holy Scripture by many names, such as, the Lake, the Sea of Tiberias, the Lake of Gennesaret, the Sea of Galilee. To-day in Israel, it is better known by its ancient Hebrew name, 'The Kinneret', the name by which it is first referred to in the Book of Numbers. This name is derived from 'kinnor', a Jewish harp, and reflects the shape of the lake. This precious jewel set amongst the surrounding hills, covers an area of 170 sq km. Its greatest width is 13km and its length is 21km. It is 212 metres below the level of the Mediterranean. It is the only fresh water lake in Israel.

To-day, just one city, Tiberias, remains by the lake - a city founded in about A.D. 20 by Herod Antipas, son of Herod the Great. He named it in honour of the Roman Emperor. Tiberias became the centre of Rabbinic learning, and the seat of the Sanhedrin after the fall of Jerusalem and the destruction of the Temple in A.D. 70.

Our main interest lies in the several holy sites further around the lake. We leave Tiberias and travel northwards along the western shore. Soon we pass some ancient ruins on our right, in between the road and the lake - the ruins of Magdala.

The Magdalene we shall always remember is, of course, Mary. Mary experienced a wonderful healing by Jesus, and was the first person to see Him after His Resurrection. Leaving Magdala, we have a beautiful drive across the Plain of Ginnosar, through the banana plantations of the Kibbutz. It is here in Kibbutz Ginnosar that the 'Jesus Boat' is on display. The discovery of this boat in 1986 near Magdala created great excitement throughout the world. It is 9m in length, 2.5 m wide and 1.25m high. It was, without any doubt, in use as a fishing vessel during the 1st century A.D.

Soon we reach our first stop. This is on a hilltop overlooking the lake. It is known simply as the Mount of Beatitudes, for it was on this hillside that Jesus delivered the Sermon on the Mount. We walk through the gates of the compound and enter a world of peace and beauty. The gardens, together with its flowerbeds and terraces, all add to the tranquillity of the place. In the centre rises 'an architectural essay in atmosphere and symbolism' - a splendid church, a fitting masterpiece to reflect the eternal truths of the Beatitudes. It is a modern building, completed in 1938.

Standing on this hilltop, gazing down on the blue Galilee, with the deep silence only broken by the singing of the birds, is surely one of life's highlights, never to be surpassed. As we leave, we notice a plaque fixed to a terrace wall. It reads:

Who makes us happy, Jesus as You.
Therefore my heart rejoices in You,
Jesus, O Joy eternal. Mb.

Descending to the lakeside, we now visit the place commemorating the feeding of the five thousand. In the recently built church, there is a beautiful mosaic of the five loaves and two small fishes. This mosaic was part of the floor of a 4th century church. The place is named Tabgha, which is a corruption of the Greek 'heptapegon', meaning seven springs. In fact, it is the warmth of the water from these springs that attracts large quantities of fish here during the winter months. Standing here, at Tabgha, we can still hear the command of Jesus that He gave to the disciples following this miracle, "Gather up the fragments that remain, that nothing be lost." Surely this command of Jesus has a meaningful human application in our world to-day - human fragments, the ones and twos, the lonely.

Adjoining this site is one known as 'Mensa Christi', the place where Jesus met His disciples after the resurrection. We walk down to the lakeside and recall that wonderful morning scene. The description by John is so vivid that we can easily relive the historic meeting. The disciples had toiled all night but had caught nothing. Coming back to land so disconsolately, they observe Someone on the shore. "It is the Lord" declares John, and so it was. Then, at His command, they return out to sea and let down the nets once again and this time they catch a bumper harvest.

Now one last visit before we return to Tiberias.   This is to the town of
Jesus - the town called Kfar Nahum, which we know as Capernaum.   This
city, with Chorazim and Bethsaida, came under the condemnation of Jesus.
All three are ruins to-day.   Capernaum was a proud city.   It was situated on
the Imperial Highway to Damascus - a border town with both a customs post
and a military garrison.   It was here that Jesus paid the Temple tax.   Here He
called His first disciples.   It was here in Capernaum that He gave the famous
discourse on the Bread of Life.   Jesus settled here after leaving Nazareth.
Peter lived here and it was here that Jesus healed Peter's mother in law.   At the
city gates, 'at even ere the sun did set', Jesus healed the sick.   In 1990, a new
church was opened, built over the site of the house of Peter.

Surveying the ruins of these Galilean towns, Chorazim, Bethsaida and
Capernaum, I feel that they are landmarks set here by God as a warning for
future generations, as to judgment to come.   Some years ago, a town in the
U.S.A.  was at a loss to know how to stop the traffic carnage within its bor-
ders on State holidays.   A main highway passed through the centre of the
town .  Despite notices, speed limits etc., the loss of life continued.   Nothing
would slow the speed of traffic.   At last an idea surfaced.   On the eve of
national holidays, they pulled out an old wreck on to the verge of town, and
then smothered it with fresh red paint.   Accidents were reduced at once!! Car
drivers slowed down to look aghast at the seemingly fresh accident, and then
crawled through the town.

These Galilean towns also serve as warnings.   They emphasise that with
privilege comes responsibility.   These towns had experienced the power of
Christ.   These towns had experienced the blessings of Christ.   *But* these towns
had rejected the message of Christ.

Does this not ring a bell with us - not only in our national life but also in
our own personal life?   These towns had rejected the message through per-
versity despite the patience, the pleadings and the promises of Christ.   The
result of this obstinacy is visible to all, to-day.   These landmarks, to me, are
fingers pointing southwards to a hill top outside the city walls of Jerusalem,
vividly expressed in a verse of a well known hymn:

There lies, beneath its shadow,
But on the farther side,
The darkness of an awful grave
That gapes both deep and wide:

And there between us stands the cross,
Two arms outstretched to save;
Like a *watchman* set to guard the way
From that eternal grave.                    (Elizabeth Chapman)

The cross of Christ towers over the wrecks of time and is God's answer to man's plight. There is nothing more tragic than the ruins of these towns besides the Sea of Galilee. It behoves us to take heed of the message they are proclaiming.

We must not leave this area without having a boat ride across the sea. During this crossing we shall be able to see the place where the herd of pigs ran down into the sea, following the healing of the man possessed with many demons.

The storms on the lake are vividly described, so much so that we can almost hear the voice of the Lord as He displayed His mastery of the storms. His command, 'Peace be still', rings down through the ages. His touch still has that ancient power and He can, with that same power, still the storms of life. His peace is beyond our understanding but is the precious possession of all those who know Him as Saviour and Friend.

We return to Tiberias along that same shore road by which we came. The sea is calm reflecting the glow of the evening sun. Above are the ancient hills cradling the Galilee as once they cradled Christianity. Let us thank God for those fishermen from the Galilee, who took this Christian message to the world.

# 9. MOUNT TABOR

"And Barak charged down from Mount Tabor with ten thousand men" (Judges 4:14). "The kings came and they fought, those kings of Canaan at Taanach, near the Waters of Megiddo , but no booty of silver did they take. The stars fought from heaven, from their orbits they fought against Sisera. The torrent of Kishon swept them away, the torrent of old, the torrent of Kishon - March on, be strong my soul." (Judges 5:19-21, NJB). So sang Deborah at Tabor on the day God delivered the enemy into the hands of the Israelites.

Centuries later, our Lord was to ascend this same mountain, together with three of His disciples, Peter, James and John. Here on the mountain top, His majestic glory shone through His earthly form. His face was like the sun and His clothes became as dazzling as light. In the words of Holy Writ, "Jesus was transfigured". No wonder that a visit to this holy mountain, the most beautiful mountain in the Galilee, has become a highlight of any pilgrimage to the Holy Land.

We can take a taxi from either Nazareth or Tiberias and drive to the summit of the mountain. The last part of this journey is both exciting and breathtaking as the car circumnavigates the many hairpin bends. Earlier pilgrims had to climb up the 4340 steps chiselled out of the rock, traces of which can still be seen. Mount Tabor is 560m above the level of the Mediterranean but, more to the point, it is 602m above the Plain of Esdraelon. It dominates the whole of the surrounding area, not only because of its height but because of its unique shape. It is 1200m in length and 400m in width at its base. The view from the top is spectacular. A glorious panorama unfolds before our eyes. Over to the North-East, we can, on a clear day see Mount Hermon, much of the year snowcapped, and remind ourselves of the Psalmist who declared: "Tabor and Hermon shall rejoice in thy name" (Psalm 89:12).

To the East, we are looking over to the Sea of Galilee and to that area so intimately connected with our Lord's earthly ministry. Southwards lie the hills of Samaria including Mount Ebal and Mount Gerizim. Below us is the Plain of Megiddo where so many great battles have been fought and where Armageddon, that final great battle, will be staged. Dotted around, shining like mirrors, are the small artificial lakes devoted to the modern industry of fish farming.

Having taken in this visual feast embracing so many places of biblical interest, we must now turn our attention to the main reason for our visit - the Transfiguration. We walk along the pathway leading into the church. To the left are the ancient ruins of a Benedictine monastery. The Benedictine monks were installed by Tancred in 1099, but they were massacred and their buildings destroyed by the Turks in 1113. In the 4th century, St Helen constructed a splendid church on this site, dedicating it to the Transfiguration. Later in the 13th century, the knights of St John came here for a brief 8 years. Finally, it was in the 17th century that the Franciscans arrived. It was to celebrate the 7th century of the arrival of St Francis of Assisi in the Holy Land that the present church was built. It was dedicated in 1924.

As we enter the church, something of the divine glory takes hold of us. An aura of holiness seems to pervade the very air we breathe. Inside the church our attention is at once drawn to the magnificent focal point - a resplendent glowing mosaic of Christ Triumphant. It fills the whole of the central apse with a glorious radiance. On either side are the two great biblical characters - Moses, representing the Law, and Elijah, the Prophets. Looking on, entranced and wonder-struck by what they are witnessing, are the three disciples, Peter, James and John. Never were they to forget that scene. "We beheld his glory", cried John in later years. "We were eyewitnesses of his majesty", exclaimed Peter, in his letter to the early Church. James, who was martyred not long after this, never had the opportunity of recording his feelings.

As for ourselves, we stand gazing upwards at this most beautiful of mosaics, and then spontaneously break into a song of worship:

Thou art worthy,
Thou art worthy,
Thou art worthy, O Lord,

> To receive glory, glory and honour, glory and honour and power,
> For Thou hast created, hast all things created,
> For Thou hast created all things.
> And for Thy pleasure they were created,
> Thou art worthy, O Lord.   (Revelation 4:11).

Below this central apse is the crypt, tastefully decorated with mosaics depicting the Nativity, the Eucharist, the Passion and Death, and the Resurrection of our Lord. The crypt is bathed with a soft diffused light coming through stained glass windows on which we see pictured two peacocks. The peacock was the early Christian symbol of eternity. The colours in their tail feathers never fade.

Before leaving the Church, we visit the two chapels dedicated to Moses and Elijah. Moses is shown on Mount Sinai holding the tablets of the Law, and Elijah is shown on Mount Carmel between the two altars as he confronts the priests of Baal. Turning, we take one last look at that central tableau of intrinsic beauty. We recall how it all ended for the three disciples on that memorable day: "Suddenly a bright cloud covered them with shadow and suddenly from the cloud there came a voice which said, 'This is my Son, the Beloved. He enjoys my favour. Listen to Him'. When they heard this, the disciples fell on their faces with fear. But Jesus came up and touched them saying, 'Do not be afraid' - and when they raised their eyes, they saw no one but Jesus".

Quietly we leave the church, rejoin the taxi, and begin the long descent to the plain below. How right Guerin was when he said, "Tabor rises up to heaven like an altar that the Creator built to Himself". Comments Hoade, "It is the greatest altar in the greatest sanctuary of the world."

# 10. CANA OF GALILEE.

The wedding at Cana stands out in our memories as the occasion when the water was turned into wine. It is important because this was the first miracle of the Lord Jesus - a sign that He had come from God. It was the first occasion in which He manifested His glory. The Bible tells us that the wedding took place on the third day.

When God created the world, He never gave names to the days of the week. He called them by numbers. This is still adhered to in modern Israel. It would therefore be quite logical to infer from this that the wedding at Cana took place on a Tuesday, the third day. This is interesting because many Jewish people are married either on the third day or the sixth day - that is either Tuesday or Friday. The reason for this is to be found in the opening chapter of the book of Genesis. During the work of creation, the third day and the sixth day stand out. On each day, God pronounces that His work was good. However, on the third day, He twice declares the work to be good. On the sixth day, God declares all that He had made to be "very good". What better days to choose for a marriage!!

The apostle John in writing his Gospel has a definite objective in mind: "These are written, that ye might believe that Jesus is the Messiah, the Son of God; and that believing ye might have life through his name" (20:31). I love the way Watchman Nee puts it. He reminds us that when a big Pentecostal catch was needed, the Lord chooses as His servant...the big fisherman to fulfil the task. When new churches had to be planted, a tent maker is chosen. Then when holes began to appear in the fabric of the early Church, a net mender is chosen, the apostle John (Matthew 4:21).

There are no parables in this fourth Gospel, no long narrative, interspersed with countless miracles. John with his clear objective in mind and under the guidance of the Holy Spirit, selects just seven signs to emphasise beyond all doubt that the Lord Jesus was the Messiah, the Son of God.

Seven signs! How significant this is.  Seven, Sheva in Hebrew, is the divine mystical number.  It also has the meaning of a covenant, as in Beer Sheva, the well of the covenant.  Seven speaks of perfection, completeness, generally in what is divine.  There are 40 references to the number seven in the Book of Revelation.  On the other hand, when Moses appeared before Pharoah, he too had to establish his divine mission.  The Lord gave to Moses, not seven signs, but rather ten.  This number is also significant.  Ten in Scripture speaks of human responsibility.  There are ten commandments, ten virgins in Matthew 25, ten servants in Luke 19.

When considering these signs it cannot be emphasised enough that they all hinge on the first one.  The first sets the scene, as it were, for what is to follow.  It lays down the pattern that the remainder will follow.  It provides the backcloth to the overall ministry and purpose of the mission.

The mission of Moses was one of impending judgment. "Let my people go." Should Pharoah ignore the message, then divine retribution will follow. The first sign of Moses bears this out: "All the waters that were in the river were turned to blood" (Exodus 7:20).  Blood speaks of death and judgment. This is to be the outcome, should Pharoah reject the message.  Water into blood, the keynote of the mission to Pharoah.  A chilling first sign!

When our Blessed Lord came to Cana, here He performs His first sign. What do we see? The water is turned, not into blood, but into wine.  Wine speaks of blessing and joy.  The Lord on another occasion declared, "I came not to judge the world, but to save the world" (John 12:47).  Hence this first sign at Cana was to set the pattern of the Lord's ministry.

John has very much in mind the comparison between the Lord and Moses.  In John 1: 17, we read "For the law was given by Moses, but grace and truth came by Jesus Christ".  Again, in ch. 3, we have mention of the serpent in the wilderness being lifted up by Moses, and the fact of the Son of man being lifted up.  Interestingly enough, we take note that the tenth sign of Moses was indeed death and judgment...death to the firstborn. The seventh sign of our Lord was to bring life to Lazarus.  Having said all this about the seven signs, it must be stressed that these signs were made before Calvary.

There is, in fact, an eighth sign after the resurrection, recorded in John 21.  The numeral 8 in Scripture speaks of new beginnings, the Eternal Day. It is not surprising therefore that, in this final chapter of John, we have a beautiful picture of the dawning of the Eternal Day. We meet the toilers of the night, typical of this world's long night. They are coming home with a full catch, having obeyed the Lord's commands. The catch is complete, not one is missing. On the shore waiting to welcome them is the Risen Lord.

I am so often reminded of the words of that dear saint of God, the American blind poetess, authoress of 8000 hymns, Fanny Crosby. Anticipating that ecstatic moment when her blind eyes would receive their sight, she exclaims:

> I shall see...Him face to face.
> And tell the story - saved by grace.

In 1915, at the age of 95, she received her sight in the land of eternal day and she, too, was "Safe in the arms of Jesus".

Cana is one of those places that we shall never forget. Now, as we take our leave, we hear again the advice of Mary the mother of our Lord - advice that comes ever afresh to us down through the intervening years: "Whatsoever he saith unto you, do it". May we have the grace and strength always to respond.

# 11. EN GEDI

Visiting En Gedi entails a long drive from Jerusalem, travelling down the Jericho Road, and then turning right along the barren coast of the Dead Sea. The oasis can be quickly recognised. A vivid splash of green together with date palms greet you as you eventually round what seems to have been an interminable number of bends. The Dead Sea is on your left, and towering rocky cliffs rise steeply to your right. Perhaps there is no other biblical site that is as capable as En Gedi in delivering such powerful sermons. Not just one, but four! One for each time this place is mentioned in the Bible.

In this chapter we shall concentrate on the teaching emanating from En Gedi. As we consider the four Bible references, we shall find that they lend themselves to four easy to remember headings. We shall think of En Gedi, as:

| | |
|---|---|
| The hiding place | 1 Samuel 23:29 |
| The testing place | 2 Chronicles 20:2 |
| The resting place | Song of Solomon 1:14 |
| The living place | Ezekiel 47:10. |

**The hiding place**
David needed a safe place in which to hide from the evil intentions of King Saul. David knew the layout of the land and its possibilities. The one place he had confidence in was En Gedi. "And David went up from thence, and dwelt in strongholds at En-gedi" (1 Samuel 23:29).

Two artists were once asked to paint a picture depicting their concept of 'Shalom'. The first artist painted the Sea of Galilee in one of its most tranquil of moods. Not a ripple on the surface of the water, not a leaf stirring, not a breath of wind. The whole area bathed in the warmth of the sun, shining out of a deep blue sky. The other artist unveiled his canvas and revealed a painting of the English Channel in one of its wildest moods. The gale force winds whipped mountainous waves into a frenzy. These waves were shown pounding the white cliffs of Dover in their fury. At the same time, it was obvious from the painting that there was also a violent thunderstorm in progress with its accompanying torrential rain.

'Shalom' could be easily discernible in the first presentation, but where could it be found in the second? Examining the canvas carefully, the keen eyed observer would have seen a sea gull resting in a cleft in the rocky cliff - feathers dry and not even ruffled, despite the severity of the storm. In fact, this small bird was experiencing true 'Shalom'. It is this latter painting that illustrates David at En Gedi. It also aptly illustrates the child of God, who has put his complete trust in his Heavenly Father.

Anna Waring puts it so clearly in her well known hymn, 'In heavenly love abiding':

> The storm may roar without me.
> My heart may low be laid.
> But God is round about me.
> And can I be dismayed?

William Cushing expresses it in similar vein:

> In the tempests of life, on its wide heaving sea,
> Thou Blest Rock of Ages, I'm hiding in Thee.

The cross of Christ is our En Gedi - the shadow of a mighty rock within a weary land. Corrie Ten Boom once said "His will is our hiding place". It is in this shelter that we can experience true Shalom, true peace.

The Christian believer has no need to seek a desert monastery, a place of escape from a hostile world. En Gedi, the hiding place, proclaims to us that in a world of storm, conflict and uncertainties, we can know the 'peace of God that passeth all understanding'. Whatever may transpire, our peace is secure.

We can be just like the little seagull - surrounded by a storm that could be causing many a shipwreck - and yet having that inward peace. "Rock of Ages", said Toplady, "Let me hide myself in Thee". The Apostle Paul said: "For I am persuaded, that neither death, nor life, nor angels, nor principalities, nor powers, nor things present, nor things to come, nor height, nor depth, nor any other creature shall be able to separate us from the love of God, which is in Christ Jesus our Lord" (Romans 8:38,39). En Gedi is the Hiding Place. May we find that all it represents finds a reflection in our own life.

### The testing place

Alarm bells are ringing over Jerusalem! The enemy is on its way to attack the city.

"Then there came some that told Jehoshaphat, saying, There cometh a great multitude against thee from beyond the sea on this side Syria; and, behold they be in...En-gedi" (2 Chronicles 20:2).

What follows is a divine blueprint for every church fellowship threatened by an attack from Satanic forces, or for that matter from within the wider church community. It is not just a matter of what the king did, but what he did not do, when he received the report. The enemy is marshalling his forces at En Gedi and preparing to march on Jerusalem. The king at once mobilises his army...flies into a panic...prepares for a siege...seeks external help...No, not a bit of it! The king, at once, calls a prayer meeting and proclaims a fast.

The wonderful thing is that we have a partial transcript of that meeting. This is such a help as it provides us with guidelines when we are in similar circumstances. In some aspects, the prayer meeting is conducted along very similar lines to the one recorded in Acts 4: 23-31. We read that they gathered together to ask help of the Lord, but before they come with their plea for help, they recount the greatness of God and that He is their God. They confess their own inadequacy, "neither know we what to do: but our eyes are upon thee" (v.12).

Then, as they wait upon the Lord, a brother stands up and declares that he has a word from the Lord. He tells them that they are not to be afraid, for the battle is not theirs but God's. "Ye shall not need to fight...stand ye still and see the salvation of the LORD". The tragedy to-day is that should a word like this be given in a prayer meeting, it is so often quietly ignored.

The reaction here is most instructive. The company accepted the prophetic word and terminated the prayer meeting, as prayer was now no longer necessary. Instead they turned the prayer meeting into a worship and praise meeting. Then to bed and to sleep, and an early rising in the morning. In the cold light of a new day, how would they appraise the situation? The enemy was still very much alive at En Gedi and threatening Jerusalem. Nothing had altered but for the fact that they had had a word from the Lord. When would God step in and act?

Here we have a wonderful divine principle. When God promises us something, He expects us to act in faith, to show that we are prepared to take Him at His word. God will then honour our faith. When Joshua was to lead the children of Israel into the promised land, the river Jordan stood in the way. God told them to cross, but the water never gave way *until* the priests got their feet wet. If they had stayed on the bank, nothing would have happened.

Now on the occasion before us, it would appear that God is waiting to see whether the king and the people would really take Him at His word. The biblical account is so vivid : "[The king] appointed singers unto the LORD, and that should praise the beauty of holiness, as they went out *before* the army, and to say, Praise the LORD; for his mercy endureth for ever" (2 Chronicles 20:21). "And when they began to sing and to praise, the LORD set ambushments against the [opposing forces]" (v.22).

The result - a defeated enemy; praising and joyful inhabitants of Jerusalem and all Judah. A great celebration is held in a valley, a few miles from Jerusalem. The valley is still called to this day, the Valley of Blessing, 'Berachah'. The king then leads his people back to the Holy City, and "they came...with psalteries and harps and trumpets unto the house of the LORD." So the realm was quiet, for God gave him rest round about.

Here then is God's blueprint for difficult times. Resort to prayer is the first vital step... but prayer in a positive way. So many prayer meetings adopt the buckshot approach - letting fly with random firing, spraying the heavens with a multitude of requests, believing that in so doing something will be hit. Positive prayer, on the other hand, is akin to rifle shooting. Each participant aims carefully at the same target. One subject at a time until the Holy Spirit confirms an answer, one way or another. It may be that the matter is not solved but it is to be placed on hold. Even Daniel had to wait 21 days for an answer due to hostile activity in the heavens (Daniel 10:13).

Always be prepared and willing to turn the prayer meeting into one of praise and worship. C. H. Spurgeon said:

Prayers and praises go in pairs.
They have praises, who have prayers.

In our chapter, many hours passed between the promise of victory and its actuality. Let no doubt be harboured, but rather a spirit of quiet, of trust and thankfulness.

*But* be prepared and ready to get wet feet. However, never confuse presumption with faith. If the priests in Joshua's day had purely acted presumptiously, they would have had more than just wet feet!! Following this blueprint, the result will be rejoicing and revival.

### The resting place

Date palms, vineyards, aromatic and medicinal plants, all combined to make En Gedi a symbol of tranquillity and beauty. According to the late Professor Mazar, it seems that a perfume industry existed here in earlier times. The Wilderness and the Dead Sea stand out in stark contrast to the idyllic nature of this oasis. In the Song of Solomon, the bride exclaims: "My beloved is unto me as a cluster of camphire, in the vineyards of En- gedi" (1:14). Here then is symbolised a place of quiet communion between the bride and her Beloved. A resting place indeed is En Gedi.

In my Bible, when I open it at John 11 and 12, I have before me on the left hand side, the account of the death of Lazarus. There is the frank and forthright statement of Martha, to the Lord concerning her dead brother: "By this time he stinketh"… indicating the stench of death. On the right hand side of the Bible, we have the words: "The house was filled with the odour of the ointment". What a contrast!!

To my mind it exemplifies the same contrast we have at En Gedi. There is the stench arising from the Dead Sea, and also the aromatic odour pervading the atmosphere in the vineyards. The bride can say that, in a scene where death persists, she is vividly aware of the fragrance of beauty. Can we not experience its counterpart in our world to-day?

We are living in a world that is under judgment, a world heading for destruction, as Lyte describes it in his famous hymn: "Change and decay, in all around I see". In such a scene as this, those who love our Lord Jesus should be conscious of the fragrance of His presence. A lady abbess, perhaps 1000 years ago, could write:

How good to those who seek,
But what to those who find? Ah! this,
Nor tongue nor pen can show
The love of Jesus, what it is
None but His *lovers* know.

I have emphasised the original word that the authoress used. The love of Jesus is not recognised by His loved ones, who surely consist of the entire world population! Not one soul can claim that they are not loved by Jesus. But it is *only* His lovers who can enter into the preciousness of that love.

The pace of life appears to increase, day by day. Everyone is always so short of time. Even for the Christian, the day of rest is more often than not a misnomer. It is essential therefore that every Christian must have an En Gedi experience on a regular basis. An army general in the last century called at No. 10 Downing Street. He was depressed, full of woes regarding the political and military situation. Mr Gladstone stopped him in full flow, led him over to the window sill where there was a bowl of garden roses. "Put your head amongst the blooms, inhale the beauty of their fragrance, and then let us talk". Thereafter the whole demeanour of the general changed.

Preparing for an En Gedi experience, there are four steps to take as we withdraw into our spiritual oasis, the secret room of the soul:

**1. Silence.**
We must be in a listening mode and liken ourselves to an enclosed garden (Song of Solomon 4:12) and not a public park. We need to hear that still small voice speaking the words of Song of Solomon 5:1.

**2. Stand still.**
"O God, Thou hast made us for Thyself. Our hearts are restless until they rest in Thee" (Augustine). "Be still" is the command from God and, in so doing, we must consciously allow restlessness to slip away.

**3. Sunrise**
"Sunrise with Jesus", we used to sing. After a dark night, sunrise is an exhilarating experience. When camping in the Negev Desert, sunrise was something beyond description. In our withdrawal, in our En Gedi, let us be aware of the presence of a living and powerful Saviour. Let the divine sunlight shine into our very being. We now must concentrate on His Presence and totally surrender ourselves into His freedom. He will give us complete liberation as our heart rises in worship. We hear again His words, "I am the

LORD that healeth thee" (Exodus 15:26).

## 4.  Self emptying

Only empty vessels can be filled.  In our complete surrender to the will of God, we empty ourselves to be filled by the Holy Spirit.  New songs break forth in worship.  The batteries are being re-charged.  We can readily pray:

> Let the beauty of Jesus be seen in me
> All His wondrous compassion and purity.

This is the En Gedi experience.  It is ever a renewal experience.  But remember - new wine needs new bottles.  It will burst the old bottles.  Be prepared!

## The living place

Truth is stranger than fiction! We now come to something which to the human mind is incredible, unbelievable and even impossible: the Dead Sea - an area of approximately 80km by 18km - some 399 metres below sea level.  Its water contains an intense concentration of salts, including magnesium chloride, sodium chloride, calcium chloride and potassium chloride.  It is much more dense than sea water.  Dead it is - nothing could possibly live in it.  However, listen to the amazing prophecy of Ezekiel: "And it shall come to pass, that the fishers shall stand upon it from En-gedi…they shall…spread forth nets; their fish shall be according to their kinds, as the fish of the great sea, exceeding many" (Ezekiel 47:10).  Fish swimming in the Dead Sea at En Gedi!  En Gedi has become a living place.

How has this miracle occurred? What has happened?  The answer is simple and straightforward.  The Messiah has come and has established His throne in Jerusalem.  The prophet Zechariah writes: "And it shall be in that day, that living waters shall go out from Jerusalem…And the LORD shall be king over all the earth: in that day shall there be one LORD, and his name one" (Zechariah 14:8,9).  The apostle John tells us: "And he showed me a pure river of water of life, clear as crystal, proceeding out of the throne of God and of the Lamb" (Revelation 22:1).

This final message from En Gedi is a message of hope.  "We know", Paul told the believers in Rome, "that the whole creation groaneth and travaileth in pain together until now" (Romans 8:22).  Has God forgotten the world? A thousand times, "No"!  We are looking forward with joy to the time when

"The kingdom of the world is to become the kingdom of our Lord and of His Christ". There is a day coming when He will be the world's King. At present, as far as earth is concerned, He is a rejected King - a King without a crown, without a throne. He is sitting on His Father's throne. God said to Him, "Sit thou at my right hand, until I make thine enemies thy footstool" (Psalm 110:1). This God did after the world had rejected Him and murdered Him.

God has a remedy for world chaos, a divine, complete remedy for the world's ills. A day is coming when Christ will take to Himself His great power and will reign as King of kings and Lord of lords. There shall be "abundance of peace so long as the moon endureth. He shall have dominion also from sea to sea, and from the river to the ends of the earth" (Psalm 72:78). "And he shall reign for ever and ever" (Revelation 11:15)!

As we bring this message from En Gedi to a close, consider the worship hymns of Revelation 4 and 5. In 4:11 we have a song with three strands: glory...honour... power. Three would suggest the Trinity, and the worship is directed to the Triune God.

At the end of chapter 5, we have a song with four strands. One strand extra has been added to the glory, honour and power. The extra one is 'blessing'. The number four speaks of universality and this is borne out by the participants: "Every creature which is in heaven, and on the earth, and under the earth, and such as are in the sea". All creation is joining in. En Gedi...the Living Place, symbolises redeemed creation. No wonder they have added 'blessing' to the Song of Heaven. Their worship is directed not only to the Throne, but to the Lamb. It was through His victory that they have been blessed - through His victory that En Gedi has become a Living Place.

The third hymn is in 5:12, and it has seven strands. The number 7 suggests that this song is complete and that it is very special. It is addressed not just to the Lamb...but to the Lamb that was slain. The singers are those who have been redeemed by the blood of the Lamb, and so it is to the Lamb bearing the marks of His passion, that they address their worship.

Mrs Cousins, in her long poem entitled "The last words of Samuel Rutherford" includes the verse:

> The Bride eyes not her garment,
> But her dear Bridegroom's face.

I shall not gaze on glory
But on my King of grace.
Not on the crown He gifteth,
But on His pierced hand.
The Lamb is all the glory
Of Immanuel's Land.

The song of worship from the redeemed has had three further strands added:

Riches...are ascribed to the One who, though rich beyond all splendour, became poor so that we through His poverty might become rich.

Wisdom...is attributed to Him who was ridiculed and whose death upon a cross was deemed foolishness.

Strength...remembering the utter weakness endured when it is recorded that His strength had "dried up like a potsherd" (Psalm 22:15).

This is the song of the redeemed whose number was ten thousand times ten thousand and thousands of thousands.

En Gedi spans our entire Christian experience - from the outset when we took refuge in the Rock of Ages, to those times of testing , when we felt overwhelmed by enemy forces. Then to those essential moments of precious communion and finally looking forward to the future hope. It is this future hope which is beautifully summed up by Helena Von Poseck:-

Thou, Thou art worthy Lord,
Of glad untiring praise;
The Lamb once slain shall be adored
Through everlasting days.
Heaven's vault with praise shall ring
Louder and yet more loud;
Millions of saints Thy worth shall sing
Each heart in worship bowed.

Worthy! again, again-
Angels with saints combine,
Ascribing to the Lamb once slain
Wisdom and power divine.
The tide shall still roll on,

That tide of endless praise,
Till every creature to Thy throne
Its voice in blessing raise.

O Lord, the glad new song
Is ours e'en here to sing;
With loyal heart and joyful tongue
We now our homage bring.
"WORTHY" WE CRY AGAIN,
"WORTHY FOR EVERMORE!"
AND AT THY FEET, O LAMB ONCE SLAIN,
WE WORSHIP, WE ADORE.

# 12. NAZARETH

"And [Jesus] came and dwelt in a city called Nazareth: that it might be fulfilled which was spoken by the prophets, He shall be called a Nazarene" (Matthew 2:23). To this day in Israel, we, Christians, are also called Nazarenes, as they do not use the description 'Christian' when referring to us. The Hebrew root of the word Nazareth is 'Netzar' and it is translated 'Branch' in Isaiah 11:1: "And there shall come forth a rod out of the stem of Jesse, and a Branch shall grow out of his roots". In one sense, therefore , we are called branches, and this, surely, is an echo of our Lord's discourse as He walked down through the Kidron Valley on the night of His betrayal. "I am the vine", He said, "Ye are the branches".

In Nazareth, we first recall the visit of the Angel Gabriel to Mary, or as she would have been known, Miriam. Here we get the wonderful promise of the birth of the Messiah. Gabriel tells Miriam that His name is to be called Jesus, which means 'Saviour'. Joseph has a vision and with him it is confirmed that Miriam is to bring forth a son and that His name is to be Jesus, "for he shall save his people from their sins" (Matthew 1:21).

Nazareth was a town not known in the Old Testament. It was a town with not a very good reputation. "Can there any good thing come out of Nazareth?" said Nathanael. It was here that our Lord grew up, and no doubt helped Joseph in his carpenter's shop. Today we find many carpenters' shops in the city.

At the beginning of His Ministry, our Lord returns to Nazareth and as was His custom, He went to the synagogue on the Shabbat. We, too, can visit an ancient synagogue in Nazareth. It probably is not the one that our Lord visited, but who knows? Here, we can sit down and recall the occasion recorded for us in Luke 4:16-30. As we read the verses, and listen to the Lord reading out of the prophecy of Isaiah, we lift up our voices in praise and worship. What a Saviour we have!

Heathen gods are perched in their ornate temples. They peer with sightless eyes down on to their devotees. They have no feelings; they have no power. Each devotee comes singly to pay his or her homage and then leaves, as empty as before. Our God, this God whom we adore, is our faithful, unchangeable Friend, whose love is as great as His power, and knows neither measure nor end. 'Tis Jesus...

Here is a message for the poor, the prisoners and the perishing. This message reveals how our Lord Jesus, leaving His heavenly home, descends, to come alongside suffering humanity. We listen again to His words: "The Spirit of the Lord is upon me, because He hath anointed me to preach the gospel to the *poor*." What do heathen gods know about poverty? Our God, although rich beyond all splendour, divested Himself of those riches, and became poor, so that through His poverty, we might be made rich. "The Son of man", we read, "had nowhere to lay His head". He comes alongside the *poor* and says "I know...I can help".

"He hath sent me to heal the *broken hearted*". Our God knows all about broken hearts; He said "Reproach hath broken my heart". He was, indeed, the Man of Sorrows. He comes alongside those who are sad and sorrowing, and says, "I know; I can bring comfort to you".

"To preach deliverance to the *captives*". In the Garden of Gethsemane, they arrested our Lord, and took Him captive. They led Him as a lamb to the slaughter. He comes alongside all of us who have been led captive by the Devil, and says, "I know...I can set you free".

"The recovering of sight to the *blind*". "And they blindfolded Him." What torment He suffered, as they taunted Him in His blindness. "The god of this world hath blinded the minds of them which believe not" (2 Corinthians 4:4). Our Lord Jesus comes alongside and says "I know...I can open your eyes". Again I say, what a Saviour we have! No wonder that Philipp Bliss could give us such a glorious hymn, with the refrain: Hallelujah! What a Saviour!

As the congregation heard His words, they "wondered at the gracious words which proceeded out of his mouth". And yet, He was rejected and they took Him to the brow of the hill of Nazareth and attempted to throw Him over. He, however, passed through them and went His way. Later our Lord was yet again to identify Himself with lost humanity. He was crucified in between two malefactors.   Man could not save himself.   Our Lord Jesus came down to where we were and bore our sins in His own body on the tree. Today He is alive...He is able to save to the uttermost all those who come unto God through Him. Hallelujah! What a Saviour!

# 13. CAESAREA PHILIPPI

"Thou art the Christ, the Son of the living God" (Matthew 16:16). So said Peter in his great declaration of faith - a statement that has come ringing down through the centuries.

How interesting, though, is the place where Peter proclaimed this. Here for centuries had been a pagan shrine to the nature god, Pan. In fact, its earlier name had been Banyas, a corruption of Paneas. It had been a centre for pagan Greek cults. When, in 20 BC, the region was given to Philip, the son of Herod, he built a town here and named it after Caesar Augustus, calling it Caesarea. However, as Herod had himself built a large seaport and had called it Caesarea, Philip, to avoid confusion, added his name to his town and so it became Caesarea Philippi. The place has now reverted to its former name and is known once again as Banyas.

I like to think that when Peter gave his dramatic response to the Master's question, "But whom say ye that I am?", that he turned, facing the pagan shrine and indicating the remains of the temple erected to Pan, and called out: "You are the Christ, the Son of the living God", giving emphasis to the word 'living'.

At Caesarea Philippi, the Jordan river comes to life. Here is one of the four springs that unite to form the river. The name Jordan means the descender...and so it does. It descends for some 233 miles until it reaches the lowest place on earth...the Dead Sea - 399m below sea level. This river rushes through the Bible, right from Genesis onwards. Its greatest moment, surely, was when the Lord Himself stepped into its waters, to be baptised by John. In a way, the river Jordan resembles the human life. It comes bubbling up in all the vigour and freshness of youth. Then from that point of optimism, from a spiritual and sadly so often from a human point of view, it goes

65

lower and lower. It ends in death...the Dead Sea. The writer of Proverbs says, "There is a way which seemeth right unto a man, but the end thereof are the ways of death" (14:12).

However, I do like the comment made by Dr Thomson in his monumental work, "The Land and the Book". Here he points out that the Jordan, having reached the Dead Sea, comes then under the influence of the all healing and all powerful sun. The water is purified, leaving behind all the impurities, as it is called back to the skies (by evaporation). Dr Thomson adds, "May we be thus drawn from earth to heaven, by the mighty attraction of that glorious Sun of righteousness".

Returning to Peter, I feel there is a similarity in this situation and that confronting the apostle Paul in Athens. Paul climbs up Mars Hill; from here he is within hailing distance of the pagan Acropolis. Standing there, he calls out "Ye men of Athens. . . . I found an altar with this inscription, TO THE UNKNOWN GOD. Whom therefore ye ignorantly worship, him declare I unto you". Then, pointing to their temple, he declares, "Seeing that he is Lord of heaven and earth, [he] dwelleth not in temples made with hands" (Acts 17:22-24).

Standing at Caesarea Phillipi, perhaps it is a little fanciful to think of the waters of the Jordan, carrying the great statement of faith, down through the whole length of the Holy Land. It then reaches its destination, where by evaporation, the water vapour with its message, rises to the heavens. It is then carried by the winds to the four corners of the earth: *"Thou art the Christ, the Son of the living God".*

We are living in a day when many voices can be heard seeking to undermine our historic faith. The main thrust of this attack is directed towards our Lord Jesus Himself. Every attempt is made to prove that He is not the eternal Son of God. Radio, television, the cinema , the theatre, are all used as channels of communication in their endeavour to publicise as widely as possible their views. Even the pulpit, at times, adds its voice. We know from Scripture that this is to be expected in the end times and so we must be on our guard.

The message from Caesarea Phillippi contains a challenge for us. We must not waver in our declaration of faith. This is the bedrock of our salvation. "For if the trumpet give an uncertain sound, who shall prepare himself to the battle?" (1 Corinthians 14:8). Let us be forthright in our witness to the world - no uncertainties...no turning back -as we declare: "Our Lord

Jesus, our Saviour, is the Christ, the Son of the living God".

However, mindful of the wiles of our great enemy and how even Peter himself fell victim on the night of betrayal, we need to keep in mind the watchwords from Caesarea Phillippi:

> Be ever prepared.
> Be ever prayerful.
> Be ever praising.

They will keep our feet firmly on the royal road to victory.

# 14. MOUNT CARMEL

Carmel - translated means "the vineyard of God". It certainly is one of the most attractive places in the Holy Land - a symbol of loveliness and fruitfulness.

Carmel is a range of hills - some 24 km long and rising to a height of 546km above sea level. From its summit, there are magnificent views across to the Mediterranean on one side, and on the other, a panoramic vista of the Israeli countryside, including the Valley of Jezreel.

Many references are made in the Bible to the beauty of Carmel, but we shall think of the two main characters associated with this mountain...Elijah and Elisha. With the prophet Elijah, our study will be concentrated on the spot known as El Muhraka - the place of sacrifice. Elisha is also connected with this mount. He was living here when the Shunammite woman came to him in great distress. Her son had died of heat-stroke, while helping his father with the harvest. Elisha hurried to their home and to the joy of the parents, he raised the boy to life again.

It is Elijah, though, who dominates this mountain, and through him we are ever confronted with a perpetual challenge in our Christian life. Life is full of perplexities and pressures. We live in an age when there is a lack of clear cut boundaries between right and wrong. No longer do there seem to be absolutes...rather a preponderance of grey areas, a blurring of the division between positives and negatives. It is in this area that Elijah confronts us with his message from Carmel. Yes, his spirit lives on. He is challenging us to be whole-hearted in our love for and in our service to the Lord.

What a truly sombre backcloth there was to Elijah's ministry!! A divided people...false altars erected at Dan and Bethel, substituting for the God ordained worship centre at Jerusalem - the holy temple. A false priesthood was willing to go along with this apostasy. They had not written God off - but were quite prepared to offer incense to other gods. On all sides, toleration and compromise.

It was into this scene, burning with a single-minded zeal for his God, comes Elijah. He comes striding in, confronting the situation head on. Quite fearless, he is not prepared to give an inch in upholding the principles of his faith. This is a truly dynamic example to us in our world today. Here are lessons to be learned: in the words of our Lord: "Who hath ears to hear, let him hear".

There are just three aspects that we shall concentrate upon, as we consider the drama unfolded in 1 Kings 18: the broken altar…the burning fire…the blessed hope.

## The broken altar

There can surely be nothing more poignant than a broken altar (v.30). It serves as a present tragic reminder of past times of united fellowship and communion. A broken altar is so often the final outcome of a division amongst the people of God. It is not an overnight phenomenon; more likely than not, the enemy has been insidiously busy over a period of time. This is both a lesson and a warning for us, to be ever on the alert for those danger signals within our own fellowship.

The very fact that an altar had been established is a visible reminder of that time in the past when first love had blossomed - a time when Passover and its ensuing songs of triumph had meant so much. A time when those early promises, "All…we will do" (Exodus 19:8), were fulfilled to the best of their ability. Failures there were, but with these failures came repentance and with repentance came forgiveness. However, with the passage of time, came the seeds of compromise. Situations arose, as recorded in Joshua 15:63, when there was failure in driving out the enemy. Attempts to cover things up, using cosmetic surgery, rather like hoeing off dock leaves instead of dealing with the root cause, led to things only becoming worse.

All led to the final outcome - the broken altar…no communion…no fellowship…no witness…no testimony.

One prime example is to be seen to-day in the ruins of Ephesus. Here was a once thriving and zealous church…but through the loss of first love for Jesus, the outcome was failure and the broken altar. We have the responsibility of maintaining our altar of worship. Such responsibility can only be successfully shouldered if we ensure that first love for Jesus is at the very top of our priorities. This means "Fighting the good fight with all our might".

## The burning fire

Elijah comes to Mount Carmel with fiery zeal…confronted with the broken altar, he sets about rebuilding it. Elijah displays to us all the characteristics of the bridal love for Jesus, that first love. He exhibits a consuming and burning fire, a passion that seeks to give God glory. He rounds on those caught in the web of compromise and demands, "How long halt ye between two opinions? If the LORD be God, follow him: but if Baal, then follow him". In other words, "Whom do you really serve?" "Whom do you honour?"

His name says it all Eli-Jah…my God is Jehovah!! Yours may be Baal or whatever… my God is the Lord. Over and above all, the Carmel message is clear and uncompromising. God is a consuming fire…He will not tolerate a divided love. Our God will not be shared. You cannot serve God and Mammon. A decision has to be made. Listen to the words of our Lord : "No man can serve two masters: for either he will hate the one, and love the other; or else he will hold to the one and despise the other. Ye cannot serve God and mammon" (Matthew 6:24).

The drama reaches its climax…it comes at the time of the evening sacrifice. That precious time…Calvary time. The fire came down - not on the mockers - not on the false priests - but on the sacrifice. "And when all the people saw it, they fell on their faces: and they said, The LORD, he is God; the LORD, he is the God".

Many, many years later, also at the time of the evening sacrifice, the fire had come down from heaven, but this fire could not consume the holy Sacrifice. Was there ever such a burning fire? Having endured the judgment that was our due, to the last bitter drop, the Lord Jesus cried with a loud voice, "It is finished". He then bowed His head and dismissed His spirit. "Now when the centurion, and they that were with him, watching Jesus, saw the earthquake, and those things that were done, they feared greatly, saying, Truly this was the Son of God" (Matthew 27:54).

## The blessed hope

Elijah had rebuilt the altar with twelve stones, one for each of the tribes of Israel. Despite the fact that they were now divided, he was affirming his belief that a day would come when they would once more be united. In like manner, we, too, have that blessed hope before us that when our Lord returns, His Church will be complete. No more failures, no more divisions!

When Elijah went on to Carmel, the drought was intense, but God had promised that rain would come (1 Kings 18:1). Elijah looks into a cloudless sky, but in his spirit, he can hear the sound of abundance of rain. He sends his servant to look out to sea, but not a thing. Seven times the servant is sent and, on the seventh, he can see a cloud, the size of a man's hand. "This is it", says Elijah...and soon the heavens are black with clouds and there was a great rain!! The sound of abundance of rain! Nothing to be seen, but the ears of faith, in tune with the Holy Spirit, can hear something the world cannot hear.

> "Revive Thy work, O Lord,
> Give Pentecostal showers!
> Be Thine the glory, Thine alone!
> The blessing, Lord, be ours".    (Albert Midlane)

Showers of blessing! "O LORD, revive thy work in the midst of the years, in the midst of the years make known; in wrath remember mercy" (Habakkuk 3:2). We are in the last days; the day of grace will soon come to an end. Let us pray for that abundance of rain.

"And it shall come to pass afterward", saith God, "I will pour out my spirit upon all flesh" (Joel 2:28). "The effectual fervent prayer of a righteous man availeth much. Elijah was a man subject to like passions as we are, and he prayed earnestly that it might not rain: and it rained not on the earth by the space of three years and six months. And he prayed again, and the heaven gave rain, and the earth brought forth her fruit" (James 5:16-18).

We leave this mountain top with 3 maxims: Live losing...Live looking...Live longing.

## Live losing

"Yea doubtless, and I count all things but loss for the excellency of the knowledge of Christ Jesus my Lord: for whom I have suffered the loss of all things, and do count them but dung, that I may win Christ" (Philippians 3:8). So said Paul, and so could have said Elijah. He knew where his priorities lay...he was fearless and was prepared to put his life on the line.

Augustine said that our span of life was like a bird flying in a window, then across the room and out of a further window. Outside is eternity, vast compared to the short space through the room. The measure of values must be set against eternity; this sets everything in the right perspective.

Live losing! Can we say with Isaac Watts:

> Were the whole realm of nature mine,
> That were an offering far too small,
> Love so amazing, so divine,
> Demands my life, my soul, my all.

This was Elijah's philosophy; is it ours?

### Live looking

"Looking for that blessed hope, and the glorious appearing of the great God and our Saviour Jesus Christ" (Titus 2:13). Elijah believed in the promises of his God. He believed that the long drought would end. He spoke with authority. He had unshakeable faith. He looked for the visible sign of the rain, the blessing, the evidence of which he had already received in his spirit. Modern day Elijahs can also speak with scriptural authority. We know that soon our Lord will be coming to receive His bride.

We, too, must ever be watching. Our Lord is coming in the clouds; we shall be caught up together in those clouds to be with the Lord.

### Live longing

" My soul longeth, yea, even fainteth for the courts of the LORD" (Psalm 84:2). So sung the Jewish pilgrims as they made their way to the House of the Lord. Elijah longed for his God to be given all the glory and honour.

We too, worshipping One whom the world has crucified and rejected, are longing for that day when He will be universally acclaimed - for that day when "the earth shall be full of the knowledge of the LORD, as the waters cover the sea" (Isaiah 11:9). A day when every knee shall bow and every tongue will confess that Jesus Christ is Lord! We live in a spirit of longing for the Father's House. Such anticipation will enable us to cope with the conflicts of the Christian life; to be able to deal effectively with those idols that seek to detract us from putting God first in our life; to enkindle that first love for Jesus in us and in others.

I close with another extract from 'Jesu Dulcis Memoria', translated by Caswell.

Come, O Thou King of boundless might!
Come, Majesty adored!
Come, and illumine me with Thy light,
My long-expected Lord.

Jesu, my only joy be Thou,
As Thou my prize wilt be;
Jesu, be Thou my glory now
And through eternity.

Lead where Thou wilt, I follow Thee,
And will not stay behind,
For Thou hast torn my heart from me,
O Glory of our kind.

'Tis good that I my love should give
Save Thee to none beside;
And dying to myself, should live
For Jesus crucified.

To Him praise, glory, without end,
And adoration be,
O Jesu, grant us to ascend
And reign in heaven with Thee.

# 15. EPILOGUE

We leave the Holy Land as we came. The 'plane, emblazoned with the Shield of David, speeds us homewards. As we muse in silence on all that we have seen, all that we have heard in His Land, our thoughts go back to the Holy Hill of Zion…and to the prophecy of Ezekiel: "And the name of the city from that day shall be, Yahweh-Shammah…The LORD is there"(48:35).

However, it is not so much the earthly aspect that fills our hearts with worshipful anticipation…but rather the heavenly. This is no better expressed than by Mother Basilea in the final verse of one of her loveliest hymns:

> O honour, yes honour
> The Lamb is now given,
> As great as the shame that once He received.
> Love tokens abounding
> And honours surround Him
> From those who adore Him,
> Whom God calls His own.

May the joy and prospect of that day serve as an encouragement, as we wait for the near return of our Saviour - when "changed from glory into glory, in heaven we take our place; and cast our crowns before Him, lost in wonder, love and praise."

Until then, remember: " Christ Jesus: who, being in the form of God, thought it not robbery to be equal with God: but made himself of no reputation, and took upon him the form of a servant, and was made in the likeness of men: and being found in fashion as a man, he humbled himself, and became obedient unto death, even the death of the cross. Wherefore God also hath highly exalted him, and given him a name which is above every name:

that at the name of JESUS every knee should bow, in heaven, in earth, and under the earth; and that every tongue should confess that JESUS CHRIST IS LORD, to the glory of God the Father" (Philippians 2:5-11). Amen and Amen.